D1047784

Learning Unlimited

Learning Unlimited

Using Homework to Engage Your Child's Natural Style of Intelligence

DAWNA MARKOVA, PH.D.

AND

ANNE R. POWELL

FOREWORD BY PARKER J. PALMER,
author of *The Courage to Teach*

PROPERTY
OF
MASSAPEQUA
SEPTA
29

CONARI PRESS
Berkeley, California

Copyright © 1998 by Dawna Markova and Anne R. Powell.
Foreword copyright © 1998 by Parker J. Palmer.

All Rights Reserved. No part of this book may be used or reproduced in any manner whatsoever without written permission, except in the case of brief quotations in critical articles or reviews. For information, contact Conari Press, 2550 Ninth Street, Suite 101, Berkeley, California 94710-2551.

Conari Press books are distributed by Publishers Group West.

ISBN: 1-57324-116-4

Cover design: Ame Beanland
Cover illustration: Lisa Burnett Bossi
Book design: Jennifer Brontsema

Library of Congress Cataloging-in-Publication Data
Markova, Dawna, 1942–
    Learning unlimited : using homework to engage your child's natural
style of intelligence / Dawna Markova and Anne R. Powell.
        p.   cm.
    Includes index.
    ISBN: 1-57324-116-4
    1. Homework.   2. Education, Elementary—Parent participation.
3. Study skills.   I. Powell, Anne, 1950–   .   II. Title.
LB1048.M27   1998
372.13'028'1—dc21   98-16484

Printed in the United States of America on recycled paper.
10 9 8 7 6 5 4 3 2 1

In the millions of years . . . that have passed,
there has never been another child like you . . .
You have the capacity for anything . . .

—Pablo Casals

Dedicated to
doing the work at home that
will help make the world worthy
of all its children.

Acknowledgments

. . . .

To all of those who stand behind us and beside us
who have supported us in bringing this forward;
for those who stand before us,
so they may walk where we cannot go:

Alex	Dave	Ka Keung	Peggy
Amber	David	Karl	Peris
Ana	Denys	Kathy	Peter
Ana Li	Devlin	Katy	Phil
Andrea	Diane	Kendall	Phillip
Andy	Dot	Kendrick	Phoebe
Angie	Edith	Lee	Rachel
Annie	Emily	Lesley	Rick
Ashlie	Francy	Lew	Rita
Barbara	Garret	Linda	Russell
Barnes	Griffin	Lisa	Ryan
Ben	Hallie	Maria	Sally
Blackbird	Ian	Maribel	Sam
Brad	Jamison	Marjean	Scott
Brandon	Jane	Marjorie	Shauna
Brett	Jay	Martha	Sheila
Brian	Jennifer	Mary	Sophie
Bruce	Jenny	Max	Steve
Carol	Jerome	Meg	Susan
Catherine	Jimmy	Melissa	Tom
Chauncy	Joan	Michael	Tomas
Chris	Joanie	Mikki	Tommy
Christina	Jody	Nadine	Vida
Christopher	Joey	Nancy	Wai Lap
Cindy	John	Natron	Walter
Collin	Jordan	Nick	Wendy
Curt	Juanita	Paloma	Will
Dale	Judy	Pam	William
Dana	Julie	Pat	Zell
Darren	June	Paul	Zora

and especially,
Mary Jane,
who would not allow us not to do this.

Contents

· · · · · · · · · · · · · · · · ·

FOREWORD • xiii
by Parker J. Palmer

CHAPTER 1 • 1
Engaging Your Child's Passion to Learn—Naturally

CHAPTER 2 • 21
Sponsoring Your Child: Becoming a Learning Partner

CHAPTER 3 • 33
Tapping in to Natural Motivation: Remembering What They Love

CHAPTER 4 • 45
Getting Organized: Keeping Track in New Ways

CHAPTER 5 • 53
Managing Time and Energy: Putting Homework in Its Place

CHAPTER 6 • 65
Getting Started: Engaging Mind, Body, and Spirit

CHAPTER 7 • 83
Understanding Concentration, Confusion, and Distraction:
Managing Movements of the Mind

CHAPTER 8 • 103
Enhancing Learning Conditions: Personalizing the Study Space

CHAPTER 9 • 115
Getting Stuck and Unstuck: Expanding Mental Resources

CHAPTER 10 • 129
Calling It a Night: Learning As Its Own Reward

CHAPTER 11 • 137
Sharing What You've Learned: Becoming a Learning Resource

CHAPTER 12 • 143
The Greatest Gift of All: An Attentive Heart

INDEX • 153

RESOURCES • 157

ABOUT THE AUTHORS • 158

Foreword—and Forward!

If you have an inner child who is still kicking, you do not need me to tell you that homework is one of the most dread-filled words in the English language.

Homework: the stuff that teachers made us kids do to keep us from living our lives, that held us captive in airless rooms while outside, in that ocean of blue air, a friend or a ball game or a vacant lot called to us like the Sirens. Homework: the stuff of nightmares. I should know. Well into my thirties I had a recurrent dream—I was sitting in a classroom, overwhelmed with panic and drenched with sweat, trying to decipher a final exam for which I was utterly unprepared because I had failed to do my homework all semester long!

Given homework's horrors, it is astonishing that Dawna Markova and Annie Powell have written about it in a way that lifts the spirits, opens the heart, and illumines the mind. Reading this book about homework and its potentials, I understood for the first time that this dreadful word is made up of two words I cherish: home, a place of safety where the heart is, and work, a form of human activity through which we can discover more about who we are and how we might serve the world. Home-work ought to be a good thing—and this book shows us how it can become just that.

The key to the miracle that Dawna and Annie pull off in this book is simple and yet profound: they approach the child who must do the homework with deep respect. These authors are not concerned with keeping the state, the school, or the teacher satisfied, nor are they concerned with showing children and their parents how to beat the system. They are concerned with honoring and serving the soul of the child, with keeping the adventure of learning alive in young people.

Of course, learning comes naturally and joyfully to children—until we elders beat it out of them. So, in order to serve children, this book addresses us elders as well, and does so in the same spirit that it addresses children: with respect for our souls. Reading this book, I had a second revelation: not only can homework be life-giving for children, but helping a child with homework can be life-giving for adults—if the helper internalizes the spirit that infuses these pages.

I wish this book had been around fifteen years ago when one of my own children, who was mildly dyslexic, entered high school on what seemed a swift slide into academic failure. I remember spending hours and hours, evening after evening, month after month, trying to help him cope with his homework. And I remember, with sadness, how tense and tearful and tiring those hours were for both of us.

With great gladness I note that this same child is now finishing his Ph.D. in a science whose name I can neither pronounce nor spell! Clearly, he found ways to stop his slide and reclaim his gifts—and I would like to believe that some of the caring for him that I expressed through those painful hours of homework helped him do so. But reading this book, I understand that those hours need not have been so painful, that had I approached them differently, they would have served me better as well as my son.

Though this book is filled with practical advice about what parents can do in such difficult situations, methods and techniques are not its primary emphasis. Instead, the authors emphasize the fundamental qualities of being human without which the most well-intended techniques will be to no avail. They help us cultivate and deepen our conviction that the child we are working with is a gifted childgifted, as all human beings are, with a desire to learn, a desire to grow, a desire to offer his or her gift to the world. And they help us understand that we, the elders, have the same gifts.

Erik Erikson said that in midlife, we elders must choose between stagnation and generativity. Stagnation means shutting down on life because we are too frightened to embrace it fully. Generativity means opening up to life in a particular way, a way that combines creativity with caring for the rising generation; it means turning toward, not away, from the children who depend on us, and on whom we depend. Teaching—whether in the classroom or at the kitchen table—is creativity in service of the young. There is no greater calling for those of us who want to inhabit our adult lives to the fullest.

This wise and winsome book will not only help youngsters experience homework as something life-giving rather than life-sapping. It will bring new life to parents, older brothers and sisters, aunts and uncles, grandparents, and other caring adults who want to help those youngsters find their birthright gifts and ways to offer them to the world.

—*Parker J. Palmer*

Parker J. Palmer is a writer and traveling teacher. His latest book is *The Courage to Teach: Exploring the Inner Landscape of a Teacher's Life* (San Francisco: Jossey-Bass, 1998).

> *"Learning emerges from our individual and collective abilities to tap existing human capabilities and transform the forces that interfere with their expression."*
>
> —MAYA ANGELOU

CHAPTER 1

Engaging Your Child's Passion to Learn—Naturally

Is there anyone who has spent time with very young children and not been in awe of the natural intelligence and resilient passion to learn that they bring into the world? Is there anyone who has not delighted in coaching those children to take a first step? Is there anyone who has not agonized while trying to help them with their homework? Almost every one of you, like me, has witnessed the delight of discovery diminish and stiffen as those children march through the rigors of school and "growing up." Does it have to be that way?

* * *

September 1962. 8 A.M. Janey Rothchild was the first one to burst into the classroom when the bell rang. She was clutching a large dead frog close to her chest. Tony Esposito was right behind her. His hands were full of dry maple leaves and an empty turtle shell. Samantha and Jessmyn's arms were entwined, their grubby hands grasping a lifeless snake, a broken tree branch, and several large gray rocks. Within minutes, twenty-five disheveled six- and seven-year-olds were crouched on the polished pine floor, their forest treasures carefully placed in the center. "How do you know these things are dead? How can you tell?" I asked.

Janey traced the bumpy back of the stiff frog she had found. "I can tell," she said. One tear traced a white track down her dirt-smeared cheek. "It doesn't have its light anymore. That was its soul and it went on a sunstick elevator up to the sky. Just like my little brother's."

All of us knew Janey's little brother had died the week before. When she returned to school after the funeral, she brought with her the questions she wasn't supposed to ask anyone. "What does it mean when something is dead? Why does it get cold? Where does its mind go? Can it still love you?"

Those questions were what prompted my homework assignment. I had asked each child to bring in something dead from the natural world. For two hours, the kids poked and probed into the mystery of death. One after another told stories: "When my parakeet died, it got all hard like this snake." "When my grandpa was in the box in church, I touched him and he was all cold so I know he didn't go to Hell, because that's the hot place." "Yeah, but maybe love is hot and so when something dies, the love goes out of it into the people that cared about it. That's why they get all hot when they cry."

When the principal came in at lunchtime, he asked me what the mess was in the middle of the floor, and demanded my lesson plans for that day. Three-and-a-half decades later, I can't remember how I justified what we had been doing in terms of the semester's curriculum. I don't even remember if any of us figured out answers to Janey's questions. I do remember getting a letter from her though, ten years ago. She had become a first-grade teacher. She wrote to tell me she still remembered that day. It was when she discovered she would always love to learn.

September 1996, midnight. Still teaching, but now I work with adults in businesses that are striving to become learning organizations. On this particular evening, I was trying to play pool with seven guys from the seminar. (They were the ones who had sat for three days with their arms folded across their chests no matter what I said or did.) When my first shot resulted in the white ball careening off the table into the soda machine, it was pretty obvious I was there for some reason other than the game. The guys patiently did their best to teach me, but I finally told them the truth. I *was* there to learn something, but it wasn't pool. "What I really want to know is why everyone calls you the 'Clay Layer,' and why you don't seem to want to be at this seminar."

Clovis took the cue stick out of my hands. Maybe it made him feel safer. His voice was scratchy as if his words passed over sandpaper before leaving his lips. "Listen, Dawna, we know the company hired you to promote this new vision thing about becoming a learning organization. We know you're just doing your job." He paused and took a long swig of beer. The others snickered behind him. "You gotta understand so you don't take it personally. They call us the 'Clay Layer' because no matter how much money they spend on their vision statement, and no matter how far down the company it trickles, it stops with us." Clovis' hand pointed emphatically toward the center of my chest, as if it were the cue stick and I was the eight ball headed for the pocket.

"They can tell us we gotta be at this seminar. We'll come. We're real good at 'GTTM'—Going Through the Motions. But no matter what they do, they can't make us learn."

I backed myself into an invisible corner of silence, trying to comprehend what it would feel like to be so adamant, so bent on refusing to learn—when learning was what I loved as passionately as life itself. Finally I replied, "OK, guys, I agree with you. No one can or should try to make you learn. Certainly not me. But help me understand why it's so important for you *not* to."

Jimmy stepped up next to Clovis and put his hand on his shoulder. I had been watching him earlier, during the breaks in the seminar, quietly moving words around on the magnetic poetry board we had set up at the back of the conference room. "We know they think we're stupid, Dawna. We know they think we've got what one manager calls a 'victim mentality.' They say we're not taking responsibility for making things change around here, like kids who whine about hating homework, just so they don't have to do it. They tell us lots of stuff like that. But there's two things no one ever does and until they do, it's GTTM and they can't make us learn."

Jimmy was a master. He knew exactly how long to wait smugly in silence until I had to ask, "OK, OK, tell me. What are the two things?" He lowered his voice until it was barely above a whisper, and each word was spoken separately, with great care. "One— they've got to ask us what we know already. Two—they've got to listen to what we tell them about what's wrong, without explaining it away as victim mentality. When they do *that*, maybe it will be safe enough for us to learn."

Let me be explicit. I love to learn. It has always been my hand-hold in the darkness. I wouldn't be offended if you called me a learning junkie. Nothing is as compelling to me as the light that is emitted from a person when learning is occurring. For fifty-five years, I've followed that glow from playgrounds to corporate boardrooms. I've pursued it through graduate degrees in psychology and education, through the professions of classroom teacher, psychotherapist, trainer of trainers, educational consultant, corporate consultant. It doesn't matter what labels were attached to it— what has always drawn me forward is my desire to be around that radiance, to foster it, to encourage it, and to study the conditions that generate and direct it.

For me, learning has always been so much more than a transfer of information. It has meant wholeness, empowerment, actualization, liberation. Children like Janey remind me that there is a seeker of excellence built into our DNA. Children embody this inherent impulse in their rampant curiosity about themselves and their world, the way they naturally follow their interests and rhythms, seek out and risk experimentation, honor their dreams and daydreams, consider mistakes as information rather than as something wrong. Children have taught me that learning is discovering that something is possible.

A teacher of mine, Parker Palmer, asks, "Why is it that in this country with the most widespread educational system on the globe, so many people walk around feeling stupid?" It hurts me on a cellular level when I think about that. I ache when I remember seeing shining five-year-olds who thought in images or were clever with their hands or danced and sang and told brilliant stories; six years later they had become hungry ghosts or haunted pariahs because they didn't catch on to reading or multiplication. I grieve when I think of eight-year-old Simon; when his teacher asked him to give the definition of infinity, he responded, "A Cream of Wheat Box!" and was sent to the principal's office for being a smart aleck. Later, when I asked him what he meant, he said, "Well, there's a guy on the box holding a Cream of Wheat box. And on that box there's a guy holding a Cream of Wheat box, and . . . ."

I mourn when I think of adults like Jimmy and Clovis caught in a battle for control of their spirit, whose only ultimate power is refusal. I feel despair when I hear someone say how children or adults are unmotivated, resistant to learning. They may be resistant to being taught, but not to learning. No one who is sane and alive resists learning.

What interferes with this natural impulse? What causes the lights to dim? What hinders our children's innate passion? Why do kids complain that they're bored, that they can't do it, that they don't know how to do it, that they don't need to know it ? Why is it that Griffin charges in the door, kisses the air, and yells at his mother, "Don't bother me now, I've got to go to soccer practice. The coach says I need to work on kicking with my left foot," but when it's time for him to write a report on the Lewis and Clark expedition, he stubbornly collapses on the couch?

Does it have to be that way? Why do we change from coaches to cops? Even more importantly, how do we transform the forces that limit the expression of our children's natural intelligence? What can we as parents, teachers, and concerned adults do to foster the love of learning that is every child's birthright?

When I live inside these questions, my first response is to shrug with a sense of helplessness. That shrug has followed me from classroom to classroom, year after year, as I taught at every level from first grade through graduate school. I wanted to foster the unique brilliance of each child, and instead I watched it turn dull by the very process that was supposed to enhance it. I was interested in the art of learning and encouraging ingenuity, and I was supposed to be training children to be obedient workers, to maintain the status quo. I taught in order to eradicate ignorance, but found myself instead in a massive battle with fear—the fear of being different, the fear of vulnerability, the fear of the unknown. I thought I was there to help children learn, but found that I was supposed to be part of an "expertocracy" whose main responsibilities were to impart information and keep accurate records.

In my frustration and pain, I searched for someone to blame. It was the other teachers' fault. It was the administrators' fault. It was the parents, the school board members, the public at large, the culture. But everywhere I turned, I found victims of the same misunderstandings about what a person is, what learning and intelligence are, what education itself is and can be. Everywhere in schools people spoke of the Golden Rule but practiced the Silver Rule—they did unto others as was done unto them. After fifteen years, I felt as if I were trying to teach children to breathe deeply in an oven with the gas turned on. I shrugged one final time and left the classroom forever.

But the questions would not leave me. They lurked in the shadows of every session I had with families and individuals as a psychotherapist in private practice. They pursued me into the adult world of organizations—-businesses, health care, social service agencies, teacher-training programs—places where I thought I could make a difference. They followed me to the Organizational Learning Center of the Sloan School at MIT and the Visions of a Better World Foundation. Everywhere I went, I found others who were also plagued by these same questions and shrugging under the weight of the same feelings.

Fourteen years ago, a short woman with flashing black eyes and a huge spirit surged into a program on holistic education that I was facilitating in Boston. Anne Powell had been a classroom teacher for a decade, but had not lost her commitment to find as many ways as possible to respond to the unique needs and abilities of the children she worked with. When I began sharing what my experience and research had taught me about the multiple intelligences of children, and multisensory ways of creating learning experiences for them, the embers in her eyes ignited. I knew I had found a partner who was dedicated to exploring those questions in the classrooms I had left behind. In our coming together, the organizational world and the educational world found common ground. As parents, we both knew it would take the entire community to help raise our children.

When Anne and I coauthored our first book, *How Your Child IS Smart*, we felt a great deal of passion about helping to create the conditions where the full range of natural intelligence can flourish, where all who are different can belong, where instead of trying to force our children to be unique in the same way as everybody else, uniqueness can be the norm. We knew we were not alone in this commitment, but even we were surprised at the positive response the book received from parents, teachers, and children themselves. We received letters and phone calls, faxes and e-mail from around the world supporting much more than the model of six patterns of learning we had presented. What we were hearing was an overwhelming shift in perspective from judgment: "What's wrong with my kid and how can I fix him or her?" to engagement: "No matter what anyone says, I want to help my child keep his love of learning," and "I want to do something more than be a homework cop for my kid. Where do I start?"

Sponsoring Learning Unlimited

This book was born from the encouragement that our readers' responses fostered. It is a direct result of the overwhelming request for a means of exploring how a concerned parent can engage the natural intelligence of his or her children and foster their passion to learn. We knew we wanted to help parents help their children develop lifelong skills specifically tailored to their unique style and needs. And we knew teachers felt understandably overwhelmed by the changes in thinking and classroom management required to meet the needs of many different kinds of learners. Because they could not possibly cater to the special gifts of every child, we saw a new responsibility emerging for parents and other caregivers—sponsorship. This entails nurturing the gift in each child, as one nurtures the oak tree to grow from an acorn. We knew this was possible if we could help parents find a practice field to instill self-trust, concentration, determination, and awareness.

We decided that homework would be that field of practice because it is the part of the schooling process where parents have the most contact with their children's daily learning experience, and so it is the place where they can make the most difference in helping their kids learn how they learn. We knew we wanted the results of the book to be very specific: for children to have some grounded and necessary information so they could help themselves when they were stuck or confused or needed to organize their thoughts; for children to gain the confidence necessary to experiment and explore independently; for children to develop the internal discipline that would help them reach for what they really wanted and bring it into being.

We also knew the book would not be about how to make children *do* homework, but rather about the real work of home—protecting and fostering the child and the gift that child brings to the rest of the human community. We asked ourselves a pivotal question, "What could help transform the homework experience into a partnership between parents and children to discover just how valuable they both really are?"

You are holding the result of all of those questions and aspirations in your hands. Welcome to what is unabashedly a "how-to" book. But it is not about how to parent the "right" way, or how to make your child do his or her homework the "right" way. It is a book about how to have conversations of discovery with your children that will reveal their capacities, gifts, and natural style of intelligence. Homework can be transformed from a tedious burden and an arena of struggle that tears you apart into a worthwhile adventure and exploration over time that brings you closer to yourselves and to each other.

A logical place to begin is by inquiring into four myths that underlie most schooling and limit most learning, and the alternatives that we believe will make it possible for you to create an environment that nurtures your children's gifts.

Disability or Diversity

Until the twentieth century most children were schooled at home, where they learned whole processes—tilling, planting, harvesting the fields; birthing, feeding, tending, slaughtering the animals. From sunrise to sunset they absorbed and observed the unending lessons of the world around them, their growth in balance with the laws of nature. The totality of the child was used. They gained a sense of competence from mastering basic life-sustaining tasks. With the advent of compulsory education came a focus on just one aspect of intelligence—the acquisition and expression of linear information. For those who excel in this way of thinking this is, in and of itself, not a problem. For them, the problem rests in the pressure to conform and compete that limits social imagination, compassion, or artistic creativity.

For others, the problem rests in the fact that they have a different kind of intelligence and learn in a different manner than the person who is teaching them. Our misconception has been that because all children learn, they all learn in the same way. We know that musical instruments all produce music, but we understand that you play a guitar in a different manner from the way you play a violin. If you try to use a bow with a guitar, and the instrument produces weird vibrations, you do not label the guitar "disabled." You just realize you have been playing it in the manner that works with another instrument, but not with a guitar. We all know that computers use different operating systems. If I place a disk in my Macintosh and it does not work, I don't assume the disk has a disorder. I assume it is formatted for DOS.

I have come to realize that each child uses a different POS—Personal Operating System—to receive, integrate, and express learning. Each child has a different way of being smart—a particular style and pattern of conditions that are natural to follow when learning. Nature loves diversity. Intellectual diversity is a natural condition and a gift to our species. As when working with wood, it is most effective to follow the grain. Going against the natural grain of intelligence takes more time and squanders human resources, while a willingness to wonder and be curious with a child increases effectiveness.

My grandmother taught me a great deal about respecting and recognizing people's individual gifts. She told me that most people don't see what she called "each other's lights" because they just look once—through the eyes in their head. She pointed to my heart and said, "If you want to know what their lights are like, you have to take a second look—from here." I believe that when we look in the first way only, we are seeing habitually, through cobwebs of judgment, shadows of fear, narrowness of theories.

Most of us, when we think about children, see them as clay to be molded. We "professionals" describe them with a vast array of limiting labels: gifted, brilliant, articulate, oppositional, hyperactive, attention-deficit disordered. But the word "professional" means one who professes faith. To find a child's gift requires "respect"—the second look through your heart, "recognition"—knowing again, and the faith to blend heart and reason in search of it.

Deficits or Assets

Observe natural learning at its most simple and powerful: watch an infant reach for a cup, a developmental task essential if the baby is to learn to feed herself. First, the infant reaches and gets Daddy's hair. Then she reaches and gets oatmeal. Then she reaches and gets Daddy's hand. Then hair. Then cup. Then hand. Then cup. Then cup. Then cup. What's natural for our brain to do when learning is to discard the mistakes and home in on "cup." Like a heat-seeking device, our brains learn by tracking successes and discarding failures.

But when a child gets to school, this natural process is often disrupted, even trampled on. We mark Johnny's math papers "14 wrong." Why don't we mark them "6 right"? We teach our children to track their mistakes, and as a consequence, have grown into a nation of people skilled at our own incompetence. Any one of us can go on for hours about what we *cannot* do. We can explain why and how we fail, which is very useful if we want to become experts in failure. But ask us what we do well or how we arrive at our successes, and instead of focusing on what's right, we're likely to kick the dust and mumble something like "Aw shucks, 'twern't nothing more than luck!"

Try it yourself. Notice the time now. At the end of a half-hour, tell yourself everything you did in the previous thirty minutes that could be improved. Point out how many you "got wrong." Then at the end of another half-hour, stop and notice everything you did right, everything that was enjoyable, and everything you learned. Which thirty minutes would motivate you to learn more, to do more, to persist?

Learning is in the nature of things. It is an intimate personal rhythm in which every movement is part of an unbroken flow of controlled abandon and trust—watch a baby learn to walk toward a parent's outstretched hands. This play of energies is not only the pattern of intelligence between parent and child, but between each of us and life itself. Intelligence is a result, not a cause. The cause lies in the life-force that cracks a seed open and pushes the seedling toward the light. We as parents can support that cracking open with our curiosity, fertilize that life-force with our trust, and provide a rich seedbed with our engagement so our children can root downwards in the dark mystery of their inner lives and grow upwards in a grand reaching toward their potential blossoming and fruitfulness in the world.

From the Outside In or Inside Out

The word "educate" comes either from the Latin *educere*, which means "to instruct," as in training horses, or *educare*, which means "to lead out that which is within." Author and master teacher Timothy Galwey explains the difference: "Most of us are more committed to instructing than to seeing someone else learn. Our ideas of instruction come from the past and involve instilling judgment, doubt, and fear. Learning happens in an atmosphere of experimentation and self-correction, where the relationship between the student and his or her potential is protected."

To explore this essential difference, let's start with two vignettes of the same situation. The first is a story of instruction from the point of view of command and control, which most of us use when we try to help our children with their homework; the second represents a new story of education through increasing the child's awareness of his natural intelligence. Both stories take place in the parent's brand-new car. She is teaching her son David to drive.

Version 1: (David is in the driver's seat, Mother sits next to him, clutching the dashboard.) "OK, David, now remember the speed limit is forty-five. Don't go over it or you'll get a ticket. In fact, you better drive at forty, so you have plenty of time to stop in case the car in front of you . . . Dave, slow down. Weren't you listening to me? I told you . . . Dave, you are too close to that green car on the left and . . . Dave, pull over this minute before you kill both of us, you almost rammed into that car in front of us and you were going at least fifty. I told you . . . Dave, I order you to stop this instant!"

(Any resemblance to people living or similarities to actual events is not coincidental. This is exactly how I, a supposedly expert educator, taught my son to drive!)

Version 2: (Dave is in the passenger seat. Mother is in the driver's seat.) "OK, David, now we both have agreed that the purpose of learning to drive is to get from point A to point B, safely and legally, correct?" Dave pats the piece of paper where this is written as a commitment and signed by both. They shake hands, and parent starts the car, beginning to drive down the street into an empty parking lot. There is a piece of paper masking the speedometer. She says, "OK, honey, now I want you to guess how fast I am going."

David calls out, "Thirty-five." She removes the paper and he sees the car is actually going forty-five. She says nothing except, "Let's just keep trying and you'll notice what different speeds feel like, and how the engine sounds."

After fifteen minutes of this, Dave can guess accurately every time. She then says, "OK, now I'd like you to guess how long it would take for me to bring the car to a full stop from forty-five. Tell me when to put on the brakes, then count." After a short time, Dave can estimate accurately how much time stopping the car will take. They proceed in a similar manner until he can also estimate how close the car is to objects on the right and left.

Each succeeding lesson begins with a reminder of the commitment and a handshake. Dave takes the wheel, and they continue with her asking him to guess the speed, the distance from objects around them, and the time needed to stop. They begin to explore many different landscapes using this same approach, increasing David's awareness through discovery in a safe environment, without judgment or accusation. He can make mistakes but never fail. Finally, they go out on the highway. Dave goes faster and faster until he is exceeding the speed limit. What do you think she does now?

In *this* version of the story, she asks once more, "How fast are you going, Dave?" Her tone of voice has not changed from previous times. When he replies, "Seventy-five, Mom," she asks, in the same tone of voice, "What's the speed limit here?" It's not a new question. She has asked it many times before, even when he was driving slowly. He responds, "Forty-five, Mom." She waits. And breathes, remembering that what is most important is to discover how Dave will respond when she is *not* in the car. He does not slow down. She says, calmly, "Pull over at the next exit, Dave." When he does, she says, in the same steady tone of voice, "Switch seats with me, Dave." When he does, she says, "Our commitment is that you would learn to drive from point A to point B safely and legally. When you feel that you are ready to proceed with that, let me know."

(Any resemblance to people living or dead certainly *is* coincidental.)

❋   ❋   ❋

For the past 300 years, schools and parents have been following the first version of this story, instructing from the outside in, assuming that we can fill up children with our expertise. We decide *what* they should learn and *how* they should learn it, ignoring kids' awareness of themselves and what is important to them. Thus, to children, school often feels peripheral to their lives. We have long debates about what should be taught, but rarely ponder how to foster the art of learning from *inside* the source—the child—out.

Parenting, helping our children grow up, is hard work. It requires a lot of *doing*. Sponsorship, awakening the gifts inside a child, on the other hand, is a form of guidance that requires simply *being*. It needs a total response of trust, wonder, and letting go of all roles, all techniques. Sponsorship involves the encouragement of a "growing towards" that connects your child to the world and the world to your child. Think of what you did when your child was an infant and took the first faltering steps toward your outstretched arms. Passive observation wasn't enough. You had to get down. You had to pay attention. You had to be in touch. You had to wonder *when* your child would walk, not *if*. The same is true of sponsoring your child's passion to learn. This is not a question of competence. All children learn and none do it less well than others.

Mistakes As Errors or Experiments

When I was in graduate school thirty-five years ago, research indicated that average adults used approximately 50 percent of their mental capacity. Twenty years ago, graduate students were taught that we used 20 percent. A year ago, the figure had dropped to anywhere from 10 percent to .01 percent. Perhaps those declining numbers are due to more sophisticated means of measurement. Perhaps. Whatever the reason or statistics, what is clear is that we use far less of our capacity than could be possible. It is as if I am given a Ferrari and I use it only to go back and forth in my driveway. Recent research findings also indicate that given the proper environment to learn through experimentation and experience, the brain is capable of increasing its capacity.

It may be difficult to measure mental capacity, but it's quite easy to measure a learning environment. All you have to do is ask the question, "How safe is it here to make a mistake?" Since capacity is increased through experimentation, and experimentation requires making mistakes, an environment that humiliates, judges, corrects, embarrasses, criticizes, or labels a child for making mistakes is one that decreases capacity. Learning involves being vulnerable and stepping into the unknown. An environment that supports learning is one that supports children who admit they don't understand.

A safe learning environment is one that starts where a child is competent and challenges him or her to stretch, but not strain or stress. It is natural for children to quest, to pit themselves against outer obstacles and inner demons. To help them, you have only to work *with* that quest in a way that minimizes the habits of doubt and judgment that prevent performing at full capacity.

An effective learning environment should be fun, because play is the very essence of learning, whether it is the play of ideas and concepts or of imagination and dreams. Without it, children lose their sense of wonder and feeling of belonging to the world. What is at stake here is how a child relates to his or her natural intelligence—the wild and raw gift of life that waits to open each moment. Whether it is allowed to run rampant with sex, drugs, and rock and roll, or cultivated with care is determined mainly by how children are sponsored by their parents or caregivers.

Learning to Sponsor from the Inside Out

"You're never going to get me up there," said the caterpillar to the ant while looking up at a butterfly.

The caterpillar is correct. A metamorphosis is necessary in order for it to become a winged possibility capable of flight.

The conversations about discovery that are at the heart of this book will heighten your awareness of how different children learn and what they are interested in so that school—and homework—can become more relevant to them. We'll be encouraging you to explore the same three essential questions that kids ask when they approach any new task: "What is this about?" "So what?" "Now what?" Homework will not only be the place where science is reinforced, it will also become the laboratory where your children are discovering things about their purpose and capacities. The point of doing homework will shift from just doing well in school to helping cultivate the individual process by which they can navigate through life.

Sponsorship does not require that you become a different or better person. Like the caterpillar, though, it does require you to change the way you think about yourself and what you are capable of. More than anything, it necessitates a shift in how you pay attention to yourself and your child.

Several years ago, there was a fiftieth birthday party for the Golden Gate Bridge in San Francisco. Traffic was stopped and hundreds of people stood in the center of the bridge, silently waiting for the mayor's speech. Before he could begin, a strange humming sound filled the air. "Listen," someone shouted, "the bridge is singing. It's singing itself 'Happy Birthday!'" Everyone laughed, of course, but in the hush that followed, it was apparent that the bridge *was* singing. One old man who had been present at the opening of the bridge a half-century before called out, "The same thing happened back then. When we opened the bridge." People turned to face him. "It's true. The bridge is like a harp. The wind plays it all the time, but you can only hear the music when all the traffic is stopped."

As humans, we have a highly developed capacity at our disposal: the ability to be aware. But awareness is no more available to us than the bridge's song was audible to the partygoers if we don't stop the traffic of our minds. In order to find the song in the souls of our children, we must develop ways to silence the static of criticism, judgment, and fear.

When the water of a lake is very still, it is possible to see to the bottom very clearly. If leaves blow across the surface, our vision becomes obscured. Sponsoring our children's gifts is an essential and challenging responsibility. The thoughts of what has happened in the past, what might happen in the future, the labels you and others use to describe your child, are like those leaves. To see our children as they truly are now, we must create calm internal conditions in our minds, a cocoon, where we eliminate the distractions that keep us from staying in the present.

Before uncovering a way to deal with these distractions, it is important to understand how they might serve us. They give us an immediate sense of security. A quick explanation is simpler than an exploration through the complexity of the unknown. Put in a box, the unknown can appear to be contained. "Oh, so *that's* what's wrong with my child. It's not my fault he's having trouble. I don't have to struggle with the unknown of how to make things easier. I don't have to feel helpless." This box becomes the place in which I can lock away all of my anxieties. It may lock away our worries, but it also blinds and limits our awareness of what is truly possible. Similarly, our perceptions were boxed in when we were taught to color inside the black lines that supposedly defined what a tree looked like. This freed us of any worries about how to deal with the blank page. It also made it impossible for us to represent the unique ways we perceived the glorious form of a tree.

What is the way, then, to calm the distracting thoughts and labels that arise in your mind when you face the unknown of how to meet and guide your child clearly in the present moment? Fighting with these thoughts, reasoning with them, or even trying to understand them only creates more ripples, as it does when you use similar approaches with your child. What seems to be most effective is to just become aware of them. "Oh, there's a story I'm telling myself that Sally will never get into an advanced placement math class next year if she doesn't memorize the multiplication tables tonight. Isn't that interesting? Now let me notice what she *is* doing well in this moment." Simply observe what your mind is telling you—"Isn't that interesting?"—and bring your own attention back to the present.

Calming your mind in this way for five minutes, *before* you sit down with your children to attend to homework, produces a mental state of non-knowing that is beyond reasoning, calculating, or busyness. It is not a form of ignorance. It is, instead, a letting go of ideas in order to approach your child, and life, with an openness of mind that allows everything in. To be in wonder with your child is to join your life's wisdom with your child's curiosity. It is to allow your mind to be captured by a flight of fancy. It allows you to ask generative questions that have no answers, as Albert Einstein did at fifteen when he wondered, "What do you suppose it would be like if you could sit on the front end of a beam of light and travel with it through the night?"

A Possibilist's Journey

I welcome you to this adventure of discovering your child's natural intelligence and passion to learn. Rather than being a passenger in a bus driven by someone else to a predetermined destination, you will drive your own vehicle, at your own rhythm. Each chapter will invite you to pull off of the highway at a rest stop, to get a wider perspective on the whole landscape of your children's capacities. Here you will find new and fruitful terrain for conversations of discovery. It will not be stressful. It will not produce quick results. Your children's test scores will not suddenly soar. What will happen, though, is that your focus will expand from one of noticing only results to one of seeing the ways you can help your children develop an ongoing awareness of how to use their gifts to enjoy the total experience of learning.

Annie will serve as your guide and companion. I imagine opening a door now and escorting you through the living room into her kitchen. There is an old-fashioned woodstove on the left that radiates warmth and the smell of baking bread. Against the far wall, there is a large round oak table covered with a checkered tablecloth, and cups of tea and hot chocolate. Annie stands up as we approach. The sun rises in her smile as she invites you to join her.

—*Dawna Markova*

"If a child is to keep alive his inborn sense of wonder,
he needs the companionship of at least one adult
who can share it, rediscovering with him the joy,
excitement, and mystery of the world we live in."

—RACHEL CARSON

CHAPTER 2

Sponsoring Your Child: Becoming a Learning Partner

Welcome. I'm so glad you are here. I've been waiting for just this moment to talk with you and your children, to support and coach you through an enlivening exploration. We're going to use homework as our vehicle. The nitty-gritty of reading and science, oral reports and worksheets, plays and projects will help take us where we want to go—to a deeper understanding of your children's innate gifts and unique ways of learning and expressing those gifts—their natural styles of intelligence.

So, where do we begin? We're standing at the spot marked "Here and Now," poised to look back and retravel the roads that have brought you to this point. You will have a chance to remember and rediscover the truths of childhood: how your children perceive the world and what they want to learn from it, how they approach challenges successfully, how they learn, what they love to create, and what they want to contribute.

Homework may feel like drudgery right now, like an old car you're having to push up the hill. We'll give homework an overhaul and new tires so that it can bring you to the broad and wondrous view from the mountaintop, where you can see the richness of your children's lives as a whole. This journey will help you and your children discover what's possible: new ways to approach what's hard, new ways to ease frustrations, new ways to enjoy learning and to connect schoolwork with the rest of life. Homework is just the vehicle, not the destination. Where we're headed is your children's future, where they will develop the skills of unlimited learning, where they will live lives of well-developed capabilities and deep satisfaction.

Our adventure together may be a lot like other car trips we've all taken. We sometimes get caught up in what's on the radio, the games and snacks we've brought along, and forget that there's a world outside our windows. As parents, helping with homework, we can get caught up in the nightly assignments, project due dates, missing papers, and forget our children's natural talents and abiding interests. So, on this journey, there will be well-marked rest stops along the way. There will be questions to consider, like large road signs you can't miss. Like scenic overlooks, these questions will invite you to get out of the car and take a look around, to stop and see where you are and the terrain you are traveling through, the broad expanse of your children's approach to life and learning.

The questions don't necessarily have easy answers. They are questions to think about on your own, and then to use as starting points for conversations of discovery with your children. These questions will invite you to observe and remember, to be curious with your children and about your children.

So, let's get started. The first two sets of questions that follow will mark the trail that led you to where you are now and will help you map out the journey ahead. (Throughout the book, we will alternate the use of masculine and feminine pronouns in fairness to both genders.)

Take some time right now. Find a comfortable spot. Think

about these questions; notice both your first thoughts and your deeper reflections. If it helps you, jot down your responses.

- What does your child love?

- What are her passions?

- What is she curious about?

- How does she learn easily?

- What does she do really well?

Collect some stories and memories from yesterday, from three months or ten years ago, memories of what your child has always loved, when he's been at his best. Indulge your heart a little. Remember some times when your child amazed you or amused you with an insight, a skill you didn't know he had, or an interest that seemed to come from out of the blue. Think back to funny, brilliant, competent, resourceful times.

Invite your child to think back, too, as far back as she can. Ask her about special times and special interests, times when she's loved learning, and where she hopes her learning will take her. Ask her about favorites, past and present. While you get started, I'll tell you some stories of my own.

When I think of my son Brian, I think of the color green (his favorite forever) and baseball caps (he's never without one). Brian has a deep love for animals and a passion for coffee ice cream. He has never had much use for a paintbrush, but he can recognize his favorite songs after four notes. Brian played soccer for two years and earned his orange belt in karate. He's always been a math whiz and is excited about learning French this year.

At eleven, Brian is really into skateboarding. Today, he excitedly called me into his room, holding up the new catalog that came in the mail. "I want to show you this video, Mom," he said. "It's only $14.99 and it'll help me learn *all* the moves. Can we get it? Please?" Yesterday, Brian spent the afternoon in the basement next door putting new "trucks" on his year-old board. (He tells me those are the metal supports for the wheels.) Today, he proudly showed me the difference those "trucks" made, swaying and maneuvering this oddly appealing vehicle that's now faster and more flexible. As I watched my son glide down the street, I felt great inside, seeing the delight on his face, feeling his enthusiasm for what he loves and wants to learn.

Another child comes to mind. Before my first coaching session with them, I asked Justine Miller to make sure that her son Randy brought something that he loved to show me. On a warm summer day in my living room, I was amazed as this wiry, energetic, articulate five-year-old pulled a book on ancient Egypt out of his backpack. "Randy keeps coming back to this page of hieroglyphics," Justine explained. "He loves to copy the symbols and tell everyone what they mean." As has happened so many times before, I was in awe of a passion blooming in the life of one so young.

I hope you find many stories of your own, ones that make you laugh and cry, times you haven't thought of for years. I want you to imagine that these stories of your child's glory are firmly planted in one of your two hands. The stories hold the seeds and sprouts of your child's gifts, what propels and motivates his or her life. So often, we can readily see our child's talents, but they may sometimes get lost in the hassles of everyday life. And we may be at a loss as to how and when to help such talents flourish.

We know that the glory stories are not the whole picture. It's time to give voice to the "gory" stories as well—to the concerns you have about your child. Let's explore this side of your child's life with another set of questions.

- When is learning hard for your child?

- When has he struggled in school or with homework?

- What does your child worry about?

- When does he get frustrated?

- When is your child most misunderstood?

- What have you been told about how he is "different"?

- What worries you most about your child?

Pause right now to remember times of fear or frustration from the recent or the distant past. As a learning specialist, I've learned that such times are what usually bring people to my door. I had a long talk with Justine about Randy before our first session. His kindergarten teachers told her they thought he had attention-deficit disorder. She explained, "Randy insists on walking around the room at circle time. He can't seem to just sit and listen. I don't want to freak out. He's only five. But I've got to get some perspective." She asked worriedly, "Will he make it?"

I remember another example from my own life. Brian sat on the couch in tears. It was Sunday night and he didn't want to go back to school in the morning. "We have art first thing and it ruins the whole day," he said angrily. I couldn't understand what seemed to be a new response. "What's not working for you in art?" I asked. "I'm so far behind and I can't seem to get caught up. I watch what Ms. Asbury shows us how to do, and then I try to do it myself but I get confused. It never turns out right. When I ask somebody a question, I get yelled at because we're not supposed to be talking. When I ask her to show me again, she just gets annoyed. I don't know what to do. I just don't want to go." Brian's frustration nearly made me weep. I know Brian needs to talk and ask questions in order to learn easily. This was clearly not how Ms. Asbury was teaching art. I knew I needed to go and talk with her and see what we could work out.

Your concerns about your child need your attention, too. No matter how many there are, tuck them comfortably into your other hand. In our exploration together you will discover more about how your child learns. Hopefully, it will be enough to turn your concern into curiosity, and your curiosity will lead to new, specific ways to support him.

Now, bring your two hands and all of the stories in them together. What you hold now is the larger perspective of your child that is vital to sponsoring her: it goes much deeper than homework, it spans her life more widely than school. This perspective is the starting point of our journey, one that will grow and change over the course of reading this book. I hope you will fill your hands to overflowing with what you know about what your child loves and how she learns.

Our purpose in writing this book is to help parents expand and trust what you know about your children, so that, in turn, you can help them stay true to themselves. There are no easy answers on these pages. One technique does not fit all when it comes to homework, any more than one approach to life will work for everyone. As parents and teachers, we're beginning to understand that there are many ways to learn. So it follows that there are as many ways to do homework as there are learners. Supporting your children with their homework, supporting them to develop the lifelong learning skills that undergird homework, has to be a discovery process because it must follow the unique natural grain of *your* child's mind.

How can we, as parents, come to understand enough about learning and learning differences to follow that grain? How can we know what to look for in observing our children? How can we make sense of what we see? Let me begin with a story from my years in the classroom.

> *As I came into the room, the kids descended on me all at once. I had been out of school for several days with the flu and we had a lot of catching up to do. A small crowd gathered around my desk, each person asking for attention in one way or another. Winston didn't say a word—but he circled me, hoping I would notice that he was there. Saundra was holding out a paper she knew I would want right this minute if I would only look at it. Jeremy's voice was getting louder by the moment as he tried to relay to me everything that had been going on while I was gone. Trying to catch my breath, I*

looked up to see Brady writing "Welcome back!" on the board in multicolored chalk. Crystal was holding court, strong-arming six kids waiting in line to sign a cartoon-laden card. Robin was audibly harrumphing at the commotion, making a point of trying to read her library book with everything else going on.

The kids kept me hopping and alive, but none of the teacher's manuals on my shelf talked about how to reach each of these very different young people. I knew my kids didn't all learn the same way, but I didn't quite know how to make sense of what I knew or how to take action that would make a difference. I trusted my intuition most of the time, but I wanted more to go on.

Even as a classroom teacher, there was a lot I didn't understand about learning. I knew that my kids had to be paying attention in order to learn, but I didn't know there were different *kinds* of attention. I knew that some kids loved doing hands-on projects and others would always do worksheets when given a choice, but I didn't know why they all needed more than one kind of learning method. I knew for myself that some information stayed with me longer than others, but I didn't know how to make sure the learning would stick for my kids.

Most of my new learnings about learning over the last fourteen years have emerged from my studies and collaboration with Dr. Dawna Markova. Much of what I pass along to you about learning differences and homework in the chapters to come is based on a multidimensional approach I have learned from Dawna. This approach has helped me to understand the kids that I taught as well as my son's natural style of intelligence. I now understand why Winston reached out in movement rather than words. I get why Jeremy felt so overwhelmed and couldn't learn any more until he told me everything on his mind. I can now accept the fact that my son Brian can study amidst the piles in his room, when I can't think until my desk is clean. All of these kids and others will be our learning companions as we move through our exploration together. Their stories will breathe life into the concepts of this approach, making it easier for you to recognize the many facets of how your child learns. This approach will be our guide as we explore Learning Unlimited together.

About This Book

The nine chapters that follow will help you to expand your understanding of many elements of your child's natural style of intelligence. Chapter 3 begins with an initial in-depth exploration of your child's interests. Chapters 4 through 10 will logically lead you through a night's homework session, beginning with organization—getting the assignments and supplies home in the first place—and ending with the satisfaction of calling it a night. Chapter 11 will help you to gather what you have learned throughout the process and offer suggestions for sharing your new discoveries with your children's teachers, and with other parents and students. In Chapter 12, Dawna will bring you back to the larger perspective of sponsoring your children and how that influences your life and theirs. Your understanding about your child and how he learns will naturally build as you move from chapter to chapter, so we recommend that you work your way through them in the order presented.

Each chapter begins with a discovery process, a rest stop on the journey, a time for you to notice what is already true about the topic for your child. Next, concepts and examples will be introduced for you to think about, along with new suggestions to try. At the end of each chapter, there is a set of reflective questions inviting you to gather what you and your child have learned about the topic of that chapter. Some of you may want to read through the whole book yourself first to get an overall perspective before beginning the step-by-step process with your child. Others of you may want to dig right in, reflecting on each chapter first, and then letting your reflections prompt immediate conversations of discovery with your child.

Making a Commitment to Learning

It's so important to keep in mind throughout this process that your child is at its center. It can be tempting as parents to read a book such as this and simply do it *to* your child. But remember that the most vital part of the process is your child's own involvement. His developing insights are the ones that are the most important. He is the key player and the beneficiary. Imagine what your life would have been like had you known how to enhance your own learning at eight, at twelve, or at seventeen.

To facilitate your joint involvement, we recommend that you begin by making a commitment to become learning partners, to learn about learning together. Making a commitment may feel like just one more thing you've got to try to make your child do. But it can truly change how your evening sessions feel to you both. A commitment to learn together can put you on the same side when it comes to doing nightly assignments.

Consider this as a possible way to approach your child: "I want to help make homework and learning easier for you. Together we can discover a lot about how you learn so that what you are doing can be more interesting, and homework can feel more important and more fun. What this will involve is talking about some questions together, questions that will help us notice how you naturally do things when you're doing homework and when you're doing other things that you really love to do. We'll focus on what you are already doing that works for you. Then, we'll build on what's working by experimenting with some new ways of doing things. We'll notice which of the new ways help you and which ones don't. This way, you'll become aware of what you're doing and will have more choices. Are you willing to do this with me?"

Experience tells me that this will be easier than you might think. Adults and children alike enjoy thinking about themselves. Most people welcome the chance to reflect and compare notes about what they do and how they do it. Our differences as well as our similarities fascinate us.

Create a one-sentence commitment in simple language that states why you are doing this together. It can be as simple as: "We agree to spend the next three months finding out more about how you learn, so you'll understand how you're smart and can enjoy learning both in school and outside of school." Develop the wording of your commitment with your child and put it in writing, signed by both of you. Have the contract with you whenever you are learning together.

Once you've made a commitment together, begin to work your way through the book, chapter by chapter. Each topic will involve three phases:

First, take stock of what is happening now. Remember this is not simply a process to solve problems. It's about increasing awareness of what *is* working for your child. To begin with, your child may not be aware of how he does what he does. At various points in our development, we have more ability to step back from what we are doing and observe it, name it, or talk about it. For a while, you may be the witness for your child, telling him what you notice. At some point, he will be able to add more observations himself. This ability is a muscle to be exercised, one that will develop over time. What can he notice? It may just be characteristics at first: I'm a good speller. I like to read in the car. Later, it may get more sophisticated: I make pictures in my mind for the words. I know it's right when I hear it. Movement helps me concentrate.

The *second* phase involves trying new suggestions. Each of you could propose things to try. Be specific about the testing period for each new option. For example, you might be exploring what helps your child concentrate. You could propose that on each of three nights this week she would try a new place to study in the house and notice which one works best. If you are working on using your child's time and energy well, she might choose to start homework before dinner for one week and after dinner for another to see which is the most efficient.

The *third* and final phase of each topic involves reflecting on what you've learned together. Decide on a way to record the results of your explorations. Set up a notebook. Create a scrapbook. Make a collage. Build a sculpture. Tape record your observations. Make a video. Your method may change depending on your topic. But, overall, it's important to document what you notice, and not just keep it in your head. Make what you learn obvious and conscious to you and your child so you can build on it.

Each of the topics, covered in individual chapters, will take different amounts of time, depending on what you and your child already know, how much you want to experiment with new suggestions, and how long it takes to notice results. For example, you may know a lot already about your child's energy levels at different points of the evening, but you may not know as much about how he keeps track of his things.

Ease into this process. Begin with one night a week and build from there as it seems right to you. Start with a simple conversation at the dinner table or while taking a walk. Allow what you're learning to permeate the night's work gradually, a little bit at a time. Don't expect to change the way you do things all at once, even in one topic area. Know that what you are doing is changing how both of you think. Welcome those realizations that pop up at odd times as your mind takes a broader view of each of these topics than it has in the past.

Follow your own rhythm and that of your child through this process. Sometimes your excitement will propel you forward, as if you're traveling on a superhighway. At other times, you'll need to go more slowly, as though you're meandering down a country road. You may find it helpful to take breathers between chapters. Allow the learnings from one topic to sink in before approaching the next.

I fervently believe that it is the clear attention we give to each other that helps us grow. One simple question, one simple task to do together can yield much new awareness and important information for you and your child. Ask lots of curious, heartfelt questions. I've noticed when Brian has even a few moments to reflect on his life, he breathes easier, he seems to have more room inside to learn, to think, and to connect with others.

Take your time. There is much ground to cover here, much to ponder as you go, much to discover and rediscover. Allow the journey to surprise and delight you.

"Pay attention to the curiosities of a child; this is where the search for knowledge is freshest and most valuable."

—ALBERT EINSTEIN

CHAPTER 3

Tapping into Natural Motivation: Remembering What They Love

I was standing eye-to-eye at the counter with a tall, kind-faced, bearded father as he was buying a game and a poster. The year was 1982 and I was working at Teachers' Helper, a learning supply store for parents and teachers. From below my line of sight, I heard a little voice saying "Connecticut, Massachusetts, California, Nevada, Utah . . . ." In response to my startled expression, Sam's dad introduced me to his son, who was pointing to each colored state on the U.S. map that was decorating the front side of the counter. Sam's dad was a little embarrassed. He clearly didn't want me to think he was one of those pushy parents. "He's just always loved maps," he said. I came around to meet Sam, who said "Hi" in between Mississippi and Alabama. I asked him how old he was. Two fingers was his reply. At two-and-a-half Sam knew nearly all of the states by shape and by name.

A child's gifts can manifest themselves in the simplest of ways; our job as parents, as sponsors, is to pay such exquisite attention to our children that we can support them to bloom in even the oddest of places. You never know where your child's love for pistachios might take her. You never know where his obsession with insects might lead.

We're going to begin our journey together with some excavation I think you'll enjoy. In this chapter, you'll get a chance to dig deeper and bring to the surface of your minds more of the specifics of your children's likes and loves, their interests and passions. Do the activities that follow wherever you are, after breakfast, while riding in the car, a little at a time or all at once. You may be surprised by what you know and don't know.

Favorites

Take some time by yourself to think about your child's favorites in each category. Ask your child to respond to each topic on his or her own and then compare notes. Give yourselves some time with this. It may be hard to choose one favorite on the spot. Enjoy!

1. Color	15. Cold food
2. Flower	16. Hot drink
3. Bird	17. Cold drink
4. Animal	18. Sweet food
5. Tree	19. Sour food
6. Number	20. Salty food
7. Time of day	21. Sport to watch
8. Day of the week	22. Sport to play
9. Month	23. Winter sport
10. Season	24. Summer sport
11. Weather	25. Toy
12. Holiday	26. Board game
13. Meal	27. Video game
14. Hot food	28. Computer game

29. Card game

30. Place in your house

31. Place in nature

32. Place you've visited

33. Place you've heard about

34. Art to do

35. Art to see or watch

36. Movie

37. TV show

38. Song

39. Poem

40. Music group

41. Musical instrument

42. Story

43. Book

44. Play

45. Shoes

46. Article of clothing

47. Texture

48. Sound

49. Smell

50. Shape

Categories

Now, take a look at the following stories, questions, and sample responses. These go a little deeper than favorites. Surprises may surface here too. Things you thought were of little interest to your child may now be at the top of her list. Activities you assumed she loves may be losing their appeal.

Hold the information you hear *lightly*. Try to let go of any judgments you might have about some of your child's choices or lack of choices. Recently, I heard eight-year-old Nathan described as "lazy." Probing deeper, I discovered what was meant about this child is that he would much rather play at the computer than do something physically active outdoors.

Get curious about what your child finds appealing in an activity you might never choose. Use the phrase "Isn't *that* interesting!" to keep your curiosity flowing. Be gentle with yourself. You may have to let go of some of your favorites, the things that you want your child to love.

Please use the examples given as guidelines or general categories. If I suggest soccer, think of all organized sports. It may be basketball or hockey for your child. Let your minds generate new possibilities.

Notice what is really there. This is not about making your child's list as long as possible. It's about making it as true as you can. Some of the great minds and hearts of history were dabblers. Leonardo da Vinci had a long list of interests in both art and science. Pablo Picasso, on the other hand, "stubbornly refused to do anything but paint." Whether your child is deeply interested in two things or casually interested in twenty-five—that is what you need to know.

Let's start with some stories:

> Helen is as passionate about whales as a five-year-old can be. She talks to complete strangers about the difference between the males and females of various species, with vocabulary sophisticated enough for marine biologists. She has talked with them, too.

> Hallie has always had lots of energy; she finally found a place she wanted to put it when visiting a gymnastics class with a friend several years ago. At nine, Hallie practices three or four times a week. Even when she's not at the gym, she's making up floor exercise routines in her living room.

> Albert Einstein is known to have made up his own religion as a child and "went about chanting to himself hymns he dedicated to his self-created deity."

> Garret can take apart and put back together any kind of electronic device there is. He has taken over nearly one-fourth of his basement with old stereos, radios, TVs, and an electric organ that he's purchased at garage sales or found on the street.

> Cal Ripkin, Jr., the "Iron Man of Baseball," loved Ping-Pong as a kid. His mother recalls that her son, who holds the record for the most consecutive games played in baseball, would yell back to her from the Ping-Pong table after she called him for dinner, "Just one more game!"

Beth has always loved all kinds of animals. She wants to have one of each! A woman came to school last year with a collection of exotic pets. Beth thinks she has found her future profession.

For some unknown reason, Brian has always had an interest in France. When he was little, he was fascinated that I could speak some French and wanted to learn himself. He did a math project last year in which he imagined living in France and owning a café. He wants to be an exchange student in France as soon as possible.

What does your child like to do alone, inside and outside?

Designing, building, drawing, rollerblading, swinging, reading books, doing jigsaw puzzles, listening to music, playing cards, writing stories, thinking, dreaming, surfing the net, star-gazing

What does your child like to do with other people?

Organized, structured activities:

- Scouts, karate lessons, art classes
- Dance, soccer, piano, gymnastics

Were these activities self-selected? Or did you or someone else suggest them?

Self-chosen, self-created activities, "talents":

- Make-believe dramas, kick ball, board games, telling jokes
- Exploring, snowball fights, science experiments

In what ways does your child imagine or create?

New words, new worlds, new inventions, new ideas; in clay, with yarn, in drawings, with blocks, with household objects, with finger paint, with metal, with wood, jewelry, potholders, pottery, birdhouses, airplanes; in his mind, in his room, on the computer, in the woods, in the snow

What kinds of vehicles and gadgets interest your child?

Bicycles, cars, scooters, skateboards, rollerblades, ice skates, snowmobiles, jetskis, water skiis, snowboards, trains, airplanes, computers, cameras, radios, ham equipment, telephones, cellphones, camcorders, CD players, video equipment, satellite dishes

What does she collect?

Baseball cards, coins, books in a series, dolls, stamps, posters, rocks, shells, driftwood, leaves, stuffed animals, marbles

What kinds of odd jobs does he like to do?

Baby-sitting, pet care, paper delivery, door-to-door sales, yard work, service projects, laundry, cooking

What pets does she have or want to have? What living things interest her?

Cats, dogs, hamsters, rabbits, guinea pigs, horses, wild animals, endangered species, insects, trees, frogs, birds, flowers, vegetables

What kinds of TV shows, movies, music does he enjoy?

Talk shows, sitcoms, documentaries, cartoons, dramas, science fiction, action shows, how-to shows
Rap, rock, country, classical, rhythm & blues, jazz, show tunes

What musical instruments does she play or want to play?

Guitar, piano, drums, saxophone, tuba, flute, accordion, recorder, handbells

What parts of the world or times in history does he like to read about?

Europe, England, Mexico, the Middle East, Asia, Australia, Antarctica; the Middle Ages, the Civil War, Renaissance Europe, Ancient Egypt

Who are her favorite people?

Friends of all ages she "clicks" with, relatives she enjoys visiting, neighborhood or family heroes, heroes and heroines from history and from fiction, famous people she admires

What are his favorite places?

Neighborhood spots, favorite restaurants, shops, parts of town, favorite vacation spots, areas of the country, kinds of houses, landscapes: ocean, mountain, forest, lake, farmlands, desert, city, country, suburbs

Once Upon a Time

Now, think back specifically to when your child was very young. Use these questions to help you remember interests from long ago. Notice how these have changed and how they've remained the same.

> *Brian has always loved music. At eighteen months, he got his first xylophone. His eyes lit up as he used the mallets on those keys, totally amazed that he could be making such sounds. For years, Brian and I ended our days together with a song, though not always the same one. Now Brian gets ready to sleep with his Walkman, playing his favorite CDs. There is a thread.*

> *Pablo Picasso was quite an oddball in his youth. "The other students grew used to seeing him come late with his pigeon—and with the paintbrush he always carried as if it were an extension of his own body. His father [who was also a painter] used pigeons as models, and Pablo . . . needed his own pigeon for companionship at school and tried to make school an extension of his father's studio."*

> *A recent NPR program featured the story of Barbara Shipman, a scholar in advanced mathematics, who was fascinated with bees as a child. She studied their dances, even performed them herself. Some had been decoded; others stumped even scientists, who could not find the pattern in the movements. Barbara's work in math has*

brought her back to her childhood love, as she has discovered that the bees' dances can be comprehended at the level of math in the sixth dimension.

As a little child, Brian loved coins. Sometimes he would even go to sleep with pennies in his hands. He used to want to go for walks so that we could "find money." He always did! This holiday season he got his own metal detector, a more technological way to pursue this passion. This is a thread I am watching carefully!

In the movie, Searching for Bobby Fisher, *the mother of the main character Joshua Waitzkin, a six-time International Junior Champion, simply noticed one day how fascinated her six-year-old was by watching the men playing chess in the park. One day, he asked if he could play one of the men. It was clear from the beginning that Josh was a natural, that his gift and love for the game of chess seemed to come from "nowhere."*

First toys

- What toys did your child love right from the beginning?

- When given a choice, what toys did he always go for?

- What household objects did he make into toys?

- What did he keep going back to even if you didn't want him to?

- How are his toys of today like those earlier choices? How are they different?

- What was one thing you knew would keep your child entertained?

- What favorite book, record, or activity engaged her for long periods?

- What books did she want to read over and over again?

- What got her energized and excited?

• What helped her calm down to rest?

First thoughts

• What did your child like to think about?

• What was the most interesting question she ever asked you?

• What subjects have kept his interest through the years?

First dreams

• How did your child first answer the question "What do you want to be when you grow up?"

• At two? At five? Now? How have those answers changed?

• How have they remained the same?

What habits or interests do you wish your child didn't have?

• Playing with fire, doing stunts on bikes or skateboards

• Talking on the phone, watching too much TV, listening to rap music

• Wearing elaborate or outlandish clothes, reading comic books

Which of your child's loves has surprised you the most?

In reminding yourself of your child's dreams and interests, you are tapping into the roots of his natural motivation, the aspects of the world which naturally drew his attention before he had any formal teaching. You have found some of the compass points that he consistently comes back to on his own. When you know these points, you can use them to help your child relate what's new in his life and his learning to what is familiar and important to him.

School Highlights

Let's expand the range of our exploration now from your home into the world of school. The role of the school curriculum is to introduce your child to the world; to provide her with skills that will help her to get to know the world and to express who she is. At its best, education supports your child in bringing out her natural gifts. It helps him discover what his gifts are by introducing him to activities and ways of thinking he might not have been exposed to before. It gives her the means by which to express her unique take on life in ways that can be understood by others. Education helps our children to know what others have thought and done in living lives on the earth. It introduces them to choices others have made in facing the challenges of being alive.

So school, at its best, is a place of deepening exploration for your child, a place that keeps the flames of learning alive in each person. Ideally, it expands what your child knows so that he can better inhabit his life and live into his dreams. It doesn't always accomplish this, however, for many reasons. But you as a concerned and loving parent can ensure that your child's education does nurture and support his natural gifts and dreams as much as possible. Start by noticing how your child's dreams and interests have been expanded and enhanced in school.

> *Lucy was a naturalist as a two-year-old. She spent a lot of time watching bugs. Now, at ten, she catches bees and slugs to study with a neighborhood friend. In fifth grade, Lucy had a chance in science class to dissect and examine an owl pellet. She was amazed to find inside the nearly complete skeleton of a mouse that had been the owl's late-night snack. This subject was a good match for Lucy's interests. Her love for nature was expanded by this science unit in school.*

> *May and her family were on a trip to Disney World and Epcot Center last summer. As they waited around the reflecting pool for the fireworks to begin one night, themes from classical music were being piped in. Of about fifteen pieces, May's daughter, Nicole, recognized*

at least ten. She had no idea that Nicole had been exposed to so much classical music at school, nor that she liked it well enough to remember it.

Brian was studying immigration in social studies and was given an assignment intended to personalize each student's experience of immigrants. Some choices were to collect family pictures, to create a family tree showing when your family immigrated, or to interview a present-day immigrant. I was amazed that Brian chose this latter opportunity. My best friend, Peris, has roots in the former Yugoslavia and speaks fluent Serbo-Croatian. Brian knew that she has a Bosnian friend, Esma, who has been in this country for only a couple of years. He got very excited about interviewing Esma, even though (maybe specifically because) she speaks very little English. Esma invited Brian to come to her home for dinner. Peris went along as interpreter. This experience connected with Brian's love for languages and his curiosity about how people live in other places, and it expanded his knowledge considerably.

- Where has school seemed the most relevant and useful to your child?

- Where has he found what he loves at school?

- What has your child experienced in school that has excited her?

- What has he been exposed to that you couldn't teach him?

- What is he wondering about now that he didn't think about before?

It's important to remember that school can only go so far. Let your memories of what your child loves fuel your intention to support him in pursuing his interests more broadly and deeply than is possible in school. Stories abound of eminent people whose passions were evident in childhood. Many of them had great difficulty in school. In studies of people who have made great contributions, from Albert Einstein and Thomas Edison to

Ella Fitzgerald and Eleanor Roosevelt, what has been found to be common to all is not intelligence, temperament, or personality type, not even inheritance, early environment, or inspiration, but rather the motivation and opportunity to follow their passions.

Allow your reflections from this chapter to continue to grow. Come back to what you have discovered often. Let your curiosity about your children deepen; remind yourself of times past with pictures, sounds or songs, smells and foods, or familiar activities repeated over the years. Ask grandparents and others close to your children what they remember. Keep your mind focused on your children's gifts, interests, and dreams, that which is at the heart and soul of their lives, the stones that form the paths from the past into the future.

Reflection

* *What have you discovered about your child's interests that you'd forgotten or never known?*

* *What ways do you imagine being able to help your child connect what he loves with what he's studying in school?*

* *How could you help your child go deeper into an interest outside of school?*

"If there is such a thing as luck, then I must be the most unlucky fellow in the world. I've never once made a lucky strike in all my life. When I go after something I need, I start finding everything in the world that I don't need—one damn thing after another. I find ninety-nine things I don't need and then comes number one hundred and that—at the very last—turns out to be just what I had been looking for."

—THOMAS ALVA EDISON

CHAPTER 4

Getting Organized: Keeping Track in New Ways

Organizing is one of those things we have assumed for a long time to be a natural skill, one you either have or you don't. But everyone can be organized; indeed, everyone who functions reasonably well in the world is organized in some way. But each person's system seems to be his or her own unique creation. How does your child organize? How do you? If your child's natural tendencies are really different from yours, get curious about how your child really does keep track of things. She may not make it home with her assignments and supplies yet, but I'll bet there's some place in her life where knowing just where things are is really important.

Talk with your child about a favorite hobby or collection.

- How does your child keep track of her baseball cards?

- How does he take care of his gymnastics ribbons or stuffed animals?

- How does your child arrange CDs or sheet music, art supplies or souvenirs?

- Does he display important things so they look good?

- Does she arrange special belongings according to categories?

- Does he put treasured items in certain places so he can get to them easily?

- On what other basis does she put her things in order?

When it comes to homework:

- What helps your child remember what he needs to do?

- What helps her keep track of what things to bring home?

- How does he arrange his school materials so he can find them?

What organizing boils down to, I think, is a system of reminders. We feel organized, as if our life is in order, when we have found the best ways to continuously remind ourselves of these things:

- What we love

- What we've done

- What we want to do

- What we have to do

- What we need in order to do it

- Where we can find what we need

Organizing systems are not interchangeable, because the *kinds* of reminders we need take different forms for different people. Let's explore examples from both home and school.

I was chewing on my last bite of lunch and putting the finishing touches on a stack of papers I was grading when Saundra, sitting on the floor in front of my paperback book collection, asked, "Don't you think it would look better if the small books were on one shelf and the large ones on another? I could put each shelf in alphabetical order so they'd still be easy to find. What do you think? Can I try it?" Saundra loved to stay in at recess every now and then to help me get organized. Rarely did I resist her impulses. She had an amazing way of both making things look nice and keeping them within reach. There were many days when she volunteered to clean Crystal's desk, too. Saundra sat behind Crystal and the "unsightly mess" drove Saundra crazy. But Crystal loudly protested Saundra's impulses. She didn't want anyone touching her piles. She seemed to know right where things were, even though her system made no sense to anyone else.

I seem to fall into "Saundra mode" at my house periodically, especially when it comes to Brian's room. I have the Dewey Decimal approach to putting things away: "A place for everything and everything in its place." Brian's motto is "Leave it where it lies! That way I'll know where to find it." Sometimes I just reach my limit and insist that we take time together to straighten up. Unlike Crystal, Brian loves it when I help him clean up. I like it when occasionally I can see the floor. But imposing my order on Brian's chaos never has worked, and I suspect it never will. Brian and I have very different styles of organizing, and I want to help him understand his system without letting go of mine.

Traditionally, organizing is thought of as a visual task. Someone is organized if he can easily create visual order, if his things are neat and tidy. Many "organizers" on the market, DayRunners and Month-at-a-Glance, for example, are mostly elaborate places to keep lists, a visual way to keep track of dates and "to-dos." But not all people are list-makers and not all people find visual order important in getting and staying organized.

People keep track of their tasks and materials visually, auditorily, and kinesthetically; we each tend to have one or two ways that help us the most. Some of us do organize visually—using our eyes, focusing on what we see and how things look. Visual is my preferred way: I love to have around pictures of things and people I love; I use lists; and visual order helps me think. Others organize kinesthetically, like Crystal, using our hands, or our bodies, focusing on what fits where and how things work. Crystal's system was efficient for her; she could generally put her hands on the right place in her piles to find what she was looking for. Still others organize auditorily, using words or categories, focusing on what goes with what and how things sound. Cindy leaves messages on her phone machine to remind her of what she has to do. Ben keeps track of important new ideas on a small tape recorder.

Saundra's eyes and hands were both involved in her organizing system; things had to both look right and be easily accessible. Peris uses both her words and her hands; she counts on her fingers the things she needs to remember, giving each finger a word, and then she repeats her verbal list as she works through it. How does your child use her hands, her eyes, or her words in keeping track of things?

When it comes to homework, Brian organizes auditorily and kinesthetically. Going through his list of subjects aloud with him every night helps him remember what he has to do; this is much more effective for him than looking at the written list he is required to make in school. What we've noticed from working in Brian's room is that he tends to drop what he's carrying or using as his activity changes. Bins and open shelves help him quickly put his sports equipment and his books in place kinesthetically. Along this same line, with school supplies, it works well for Brian to have folders and slots where he can quickly tuck his papers, instead of using a three-ring binder with color-coded visual dividers.

Help your children create or fine-tune their reminder systems by using some of the following suggestions. Experiment and notice which ones work best. Assist your children in coming back to these three simple questions:

• What will help me remember what I need to do?

- What will help me remember what things I need to do it?

- How can I arrange things so I can find them when I need them?

Staying in Touch—Organizing Kinesthetically

- To sort things at school throughout the day, create a specific section in the backpack for books to go home, separated from those not needed.

- Establish a place in a locker, such as the top shelf, as the "taking-home" place, with a similar spot at home as the "taking-to-school" place.

- Pick up the backpack and notice if it feels heavy or light enough to contain what is needed.

- On the work surface, sequence "to-dos" by placing required books and supplies in piles and working through each one.

- When finished, fold assignment papers in a different way for each subject, so you know by feel which is which.

- Use containers of all shapes and sizes to hold supplies, so it is obvious by feel and location what goes where: cubbies, Tupperware, baskets.

Playing it by Ear—Organizing Auditorily

- Choose a study buddy. Set up an appointment every day to meet at lockers or talk on the phone and state aloud the assignments for the evening.

- Carry a small tape recorder to keep track of assignments verbally.

- Talk yourself through a list of supplies to remember, recalling how many there are, and recite them periodically.

- Make up a rhyme to remember both assignments and supplies.

- Pretend you have an assistant in the next room. Buzz him or her when you need the next assignment.

- Count down your assignments from the number you begin with to zero.

Seeing Is Believing—Organizing Visually

- List assignments by subject, each one in a different colored marker, so you can see at a glance what might be needed.

- Write each assignment on a different Post-it note at school; at home, arrange the notes in the order you plan to do the assignments.

- Mark books to go home with a special colored bookmark.

- Keep papers in separate colored folders for each subject; bring home only those in which there is an assignment. Cover your book for a subject in the same colors as the folder.

- Devote one spiral notebook to each subject. Select calendars with only one day visible at a time.

- Choose one notebook with sections for each subject. Pick a calendar with at least one month visible at a time.

Keep in mind that your goal is to help your child's natural organizing system become more obvious to him. Develop new suggestions of your own by asking yourself how he could use all of his senses to organize. Help him find ways to make keeping track of tasks and things more efficient and fun!

Reflection

* *What have you realized about how your children naturally organize?*

* *What new suggestions you've tried have improved their ability to keep track of assignments and supplies?*

* *How could the way they organize their things help them remember what they want to do and what they want to learn as well as what they have to do and what they're required to learn?*

"There is time only to work slowly;
there is no time not to love."

—Anonymous

CHAPTER 5

Managing Time and Energy: Putting Homework in Its Place

Time and energy are precious commodities in our fast-paced lives. Learning to manage them well is a challenging task for us all. Every day may have twenty-four hours in it, but each of those hours is not equally suited to the same task. Our physical and mental energy ebbs and flows over the course of the day. With this chapter, you can help your children begin to develop time management skills and an awareness of their own natural energy cycles, so that they can finish homework assignments and still have time and energy to spare for other interests.

Mapping the Night's Work: Developing a Learning Plan

There are four sets of questions you need to consider in making plans for a homework session. Let's work our way through these one at a time.

- What's your child's energy like? What will help balance it?

- What assignments need to be done? How much energy and attention are called for in each one?

- How long will each assignment take? What time is available?

- What sequence of assignments makes the most of your child's energy?

What's your child's energy like? What will help balance it?

Take some time to think about your child's levels of energy during the after-school and evening hours. Where are the peaks and the valleys? What influences them? Notice any patterns that seem fairly consistent.

What is your child typically like after school, from 3:00 to 5:00 P.M.?

- Does he come through the door bursting with energy?

- Is he tired after school, needing time to rest?

- Does he come home hungry?

- What kind of snack revives him?

- What kind of snack may comfort him but cause his energy to wane?

- Is it usually important for him to begin homework right away or does he prefer to start working on it after dinner?

What kind of energy does your child have from 5:00 to 7:00 P.M.?

- Does she need to play and rest before dinner?

- Does she get drowsy after dinner and find it hard to get going again?

- What seems to be the "natural" time for your child to begin homework?

- Does she need to start before dinner in order to finish?

What is your child's energy like from 7:00 to 9:00 P.M.?

- When does your child have the most energy? The least?

- When does he seem to perk up?

- When does he begin energetically to call it a night?

- Does he get a second wind at some point in the evening?

- By when does your child need to finish?

The learning process has two phases, much like the inhale and exhale of breathing. In the "inhale" of learning, our children are receptive, taking in the world through their senses. They fill up, they're enlivened and influenced by the books they read, the lectures they hear, the models they touch, the experiences they have. In the "exhale" of learning, kids are expressive, they get active, they demonstrate what they've learned in some way. Writing an essay, giving an oral report, performing an experiment, and playing a sport are some of the ways children are expressive in their learning.

Our minds work best when we have the chance to both "inhale" and "exhale" frequently, when we have a fairly equal proportion of activities in which we are receptive and expressive. So, when your kids come home from school, their minds seek to balance what they have been experiencing all day. If they have been sitting and listening for most of the day, they may need to get active and release some energy when they come home. After a very active day, they may need some quiet time to recoup.

Notice what your child instinctively wants to do after school. His needs may vary; some days the need for balancing will be more pronounced than others. Let him follow his own inclinations as often as possible, so that when the time comes for homework, your child's mind will be balanced and refreshed, ready for more learning. Most often, it works for Brian to have some very active time between school and homework. He and I have a pact, at his request, not to even talk about homework until after 5:00 P.M. The time between 2:15 and 5:00 is "school-free," Brian's time to be outside doing what he wants. Other kids will have very different needs. Tiffany likes to zone out in front of the television for half an hour when she comes in. Don needs to tell anyone who will listen what's been going on at school all day. Lucy needs downtime with a book, and Jason loves to play the piano to unwind.

These after-school patterns are important to consider when making a homework plan. If your child has difficulty getting started again at night, begin to experiment with different ways to balance out the school day. Will telling jokes or listening to music refresh your child? You might suggest doing an art project or watching the birds. Going for a bike ride or just sitting in the sun may be revitalizing for your son or daughter. This natural balancing may take longer on some days than on others. As a result, your child may need to start his or her homework at different times on different days.

Remember that by late afternoon, your mind may be in need of some balancing, too. Take stock of your own energy. What kind of a day have you had? What might you need first before you can comfortably support your child to do homework?

Sometimes the nature of a homework assignment itself can help to balance your child's mind. For Brian, a series of recent at-home science experiments recently were energizing for him in contrast to a fairly sedentary day at school. On the days Brian has after-school sports, reading quietly might be the place he chooses to start. Realize that the plan you develop will probably vary widely from night to night depending not only on the mental balancing that needs to happen, but on the assignments given to your child as well.

What assignments need to be done? How much energy and attention are called for in each one?

When your child sits down to do homework, there are many kinds of assignments he could be facing. Take a look at the following list of short- and long-term school tasks.

Short-term and well-defined:

- Spelling words to study
- Computation problems in math
- Word problems in math
- Worksheets in English
- Reading for information
- Answering questions or taking notes on reading assignments
- Vocabulary lessons in English or foreign language

Long-term, requiring planning:

- Independent reading, perhaps for a book report
- Creative writing
- Studying for a test
- Producing a book report
- Illustrating a report
- Learning lines for a play
- Preparing for an oral presentation
- Producing a hands-on project
- Writing a report or research paper

What kinds of assignments are easy and/or fun for your child?

Which are consistently difficult?

Which are challenging but manageable?

All of these kinds of assignments need to be considered in the night's plan. We tend to feel confident and energized doing certain kinds of homework and more hesitant and unfocused in others. Winston might love to do a hands-on project and dread the thought of an oral report. For Robin, it's exactly the opposite; preparing an oral report for her is a breeze, while making a model can be excruciatingly difficult.

Brady may have no trouble with assignments that require reading and writing but not have an easy time with a science experiment. Crystal, on the other hand, can't concentrate easily when reading and writing; these kinds of assignments take her longer, but she can do anything "hands-on" very easily.

Saundra may love to use drawings and illustrations to decorate her work, and be able to do these quickly and easily, whereas for Jeremy, artwork only happens with extra time and effort. Conversely, oral preparation for a test would be easy for Jeremy, while Saundra might have a hard time finding the words she needs to express what she knows.

So, in compiling a list or talking through the agenda for the evening, note which assignments will probably take more time and energy because of what they ask your child to do. What is a short and easy task for one child can take another a very long time to complete. Studying spelling words could be a quick review for some, but might be a long hour of tedium for others. Becoming aware of these differences and taking them into account as you plan can make homework sessions more realistic and more manageable for you and your child.

How long will each assignment take? What time is available?

After flagging both the potential trouble spots and the easier assignments, it's time to get more specific with the outline for the evening. Take stock of what's typically available, timewise, at your house in the evening. Notice your child's current skill at estimating the time needed for homework tasks.

- How much time overall is actually available?

- How long is there *really* before dinner?

- How long between dinner and bedtime? Is this flexible?

- When does your child have to be in bed to feel rested in the morning?

- If you need more time than is available on a given night, could your child get up a little early in the morning to complete work?

- How accurately can your child estimate time needed for routine tasks? spelling words, math worksheets? brushing teeth, doing a chore?

- Can your child break down tasks into smaller chunks? studying for a test, writing a report? cleaning her room, caring for a pet?

One of the most difficult things for many of us to do is to estimate how long specific tasks will take to complete. This is never an exact science, but it is important to help your child begin to develop this skill.

It's easiest to start with assignments that involve a repetitive process. Time your child doing one or two segments of the process involved. For example, if he has twenty long division problems to do, find out together how long it takes him to do one; then, multiply by twenty to get a rough estimate of how long it will take to complete the entire assignment. You could do this with a reading assignment as well. How long does it take to read one page in the social studies book? Find out and then make an educated guess about how long the ten-page chapter will take. Try this for looking up vocabulary words in the dictionary or for writing sentences. At the end of the night, notice how accurate your estimates were.

This is important to do with long-term projects as well. Mark had four weeks to do a social studies project in which he was to collect and display information about ten different states. He got himself into a real bind the night before the assignment was due, thinking that he could finish the whole project in one night. He discovered a little too late that it took him about twenty minutes to get the info for each state into final form. If he had known that early on, he could have planned his time more effectively.

Time estimating is a bit more difficult with less-structured assignments, like studying for a test or writing a rough draft. Begin by creating some structure and setting goals. For example, in studying for a science test, determine how many major topics are being covered by the test. If there are three, then your child might plan to spend fifteen minutes on each of the three topics, for a total of forty-five minutes of study time. Notice at the end of the night how close these estimates came to real time. Over time, your child will know more clearly how many minutes to budget. The estimating process is important to do on nights where there isn't much pressure, so when there seems to be a lot to do in a short period of time, you have the data you need to deal with the crunch most accurately.

It's so tempting to do time planning *for* our kids; it seems so much easier that way sometimes. Resist this temptation. Be sure that you help your child discover how to plan for herself, based on her own time estimates, rather than doing the planning for her. Helping your child develop planning skills will support her well as she grows up and faces more challenges and responsibilities.

After making an overall time estimate together for your child's evening—and this is obviously best done as early as possible—you are ready to plan how various assignments might fit into available time slots. In addition to the "have-tos," make sure you consider scheduled activities, everyday routines, and what your child may want to do besides homework. Remember the importance of including balancing activities in your plan.

What sequence of tasks makes the most of your child's energy?

Think about your child's typical approach to doing his nightly assignments:

- Does your child always do his subjects in the same order?

- Does he do what's easy first, to get it out of the way?

- Does he do what he likes most first?

- Does he tackle the harder subjects early in the night?

- Does he need to warm up to the hard stuff?

- Does he often not get to what's hard?

On some nights, with a light load, you'll have plenty of flexibility. On the nights when there is lots to do, the order in which your child does her tasks can really be key to her getting it all done. There are many ways to rank and sequence tasks. There is no right or wrong way. Discover what is optimal for your child and help her organize herself accordingly.

Sequence assignments in order to maximize your child's energy. Math may feel easy and energizing for your child. This might be a good "pick-me-up" activity for when he feels a little sluggish. Writing an essay may be weighing heavily on your child's mind. It might be important to work on this when he is alert and fresh.

Some of us like to do tasks from the easiest to the hardest and others prefer working from the hardest to the easiest. If doing a hands-on project is fun for your child, spending fifteen minutes on it right away could provide a good warm-up for things that require more concentration. If your child feels overwhelmed at the prospect of preparing for an oral presentation, it might help her to do that first, get it out of the way, and then end with something that is more light and fun.

Your child's interest in various subjects is also an important consideration when developing the night's sequence. Some kids work best by getting the ball rolling with their favorites first; others like to reward themselves at the end of the night by saving the best subjects for last.

There are so many productive ways to arrange assignments. Here are some examples that offer more possibilities. Jimmy gets a lot of energy from doing one thing at a time, seeing an assignment through from start to finish before moving on to something else. This is not at all true for Sarah, who is more of a dabbler. Her concentration is best in short spurts, so she likes to do her math in two chunks with social studies or language in between. Jason and his friends like to have marathon study sessions before big tests, where, for two or three hours, they take turns asking and answering questions. Jenni is better off breaking the test material into chunks and taking a whole week to study a little bit at a time on her own.

There may be some nights when there's simply too much to do. Help your child be realistic and compassionate with herself when this looks likely. Help her to decide what gets priority by working through questions like these:

- Which assignments are the most important for you to complete?

- Which ones will help you feel best about your efforts?

- Which ones have the most urgent deadlines?

- Which ones will carry the most weight with the teacher?

Find out what the philosophies and policies about homework are at your child's school and in your child's classroom. At Brian's elementary school, the teachers make it clear that they don't want kids to struggle with homework. They encourage children to work for a reasonable amount of time on an assignment, but not to labor over it endlessly. Trouble with an assignment, at this school, is considered good feedback for the teacher, not failure on the part of the child.

Thinking about these issues and developing a plan with your

children can yield important learning if we keep coming back to one truth about homework: it is an important part of their lives right now, but it is not all there is. Being intentional about the use of your children's time and energy can help maintain the right balance between homework and other things. Help your children make choices that make room not just for the "have-tos" but for the "want-tos" as well. Schedule time for what they love to do, no matter what.

Reflection

* *What have you learned about your child's everyday energy patterns?*

* *What are some of the ways your child naturally balances his mind?*

* *What are the best ways to help your child learn to estimate time?*

* *What are you discovering about the best ways to sequence assignments?*

* *How can you help your child make time for his dreams and interests?*

"I tried to teach my child with books.
He gave me only puzzled looks.
I tried to teach my child with words.
They passed him by, often unheard.
Despairingly, I turned aside,
'How shall I teach this child?' I cried.
'Come,' he said, 'play with me.' "

—ANONYMOUS

CHAPTER 6

Getting Started: Engaging Mind, Body and Spirit

Perhaps the most important job you have as a homework coach is to help your children connect their homework to the rest of their lives. When you sit down together at the kitchen table for a night of studying, how can you help your children remember what they love, what they already know, what they really want to learn, and what makes learning fun? Let's pause for a moment and take stock of what you already know about the subject areas and assignments that naturally capture your children's interests.

- What are your child's favorite subjects?

- Which subjects relate to his interests?

- Which subjects are generating new interests?

- What do your child's favorite subjects have in common?

- How have his subject preferences changed over the years?

- Why do you think they have changed?

- Who have been your child's favorite teachers?

- Why did he "click" with them?

- How does your child typically approach interests he pursues on his own? Does he read about it? Talk to others about it? Try it out?

Beginning each evening with three simple questions may just be enough to help homework find its place in the flow of things. Asking "What?" "So what?" and "Now what?" can help your children make connections to what they know and love, and engage more fully with their nightly assignments.

Getting started each evening with the question "What?" helps both you and your child begin to put the night's work in perspective. Try these questions:

- What is this assignment about?

- What do you already know about this?

- What is the purpose of this assignment? How does it relate to what you are doing in class?

    Is this a review of a skill or topic you know?

    Is this an introduction to new information?

    Is this practice of a skill you're learning in class?

    Is this an expansion of what you're learning in class?

    Is this a chance to show what you've learned?

    Is this preparation for a test on what you've learned?

    Is this part of a larger assignment?

- What are the expectations of your teacher?

- What is the level of quality you are aiming for in this assignment?

I had been in the habit of skimming over this reflection with

Brian. Cataloging the subjects in order to map out the evening was about as far as we ever got: his list might consist of reading for science, a worksheet in math, and writing the answers to questions in language arts. Recently, I have found I can help Brian engage better when we dig in a little deeper than this. We can discover together what his starting point is, how he is thinking about each assignment, and what kind of learning effort is needed. This process helps me stay in touch with what Brian is really doing at school. The more specific we get at this point, the more likely we are to find a connection between what he's learning and what he loves.

So, pursuing the "What?" of his reading assignment for science led to Brian's saying, "We're starting to learn about how scientists do what they do. This is all brand-new to me, except for the discussion we had in class today. The reading seems easy, though. It's only five pages." His math worksheet got more clearly defined: "This is review; Ms. Knight just wants to see if we remember how to add, subtract, multiply, and divide. The first three are easy, but I've forgotten how to divide." Writing answers to questions in language arts was clarified too: "This is a reading autobiography. It has four questions about how reading has been for us since first grade. Mr. Fenland wants to know how we *feel*. I've never thought about that before, until study hall today. This should be pretty easy and I want to do a good job."

This deeper conversation gave me a clearer idea about where Brian was able to fly on his own and where he might need some support. Doing this with your child prevents most of those late-night surprises from happening, when you discover at ten o'clock that your child doesn't understand the math concept at all and you have no brain power left to help her.

The second preliminary question, "So what?" gives you and your child a chance to explore and make obvious the connections between homework and outside interests. Here are some things to discuss:

- What's interesting to you about this assignment?

- How does it relate to other things you like, other things you're doing, or things you might want to do?

- How could this assignment be useful to you?

- What could you learn about *yourself* in doing this assignment?

- What will you learn from this "no matter what"?

"So what?" may be the most important question you answer together on a nightly basis. With this question you are tapping in to your child's natural motivation and sense of purpose. You are helping her make homework her own project, "no matter what." You are helping her find personal relevance that goes deeper than any requirement or her desire for approval.

Let's go back to Brian's homework connections and his "No Matter What" list. When he thought about his science assignment, Brian said, "I hadn't realized before that John and I are really kind of scientists, building our fort on the creek. We have an idea, we try things out to see if they will work; then we go on to another idea. That's cool. I wonder what else I could find out from this." The math review worksheet evoked: "I love math and I usually get them all right. It bugs me that I can't remember division. No matter what, I'm going to figure it out tonight." Brian's reading autobiography motivated him in a couple of very different ways: "I like to read and I want the teacher to know I don't have trouble with it. But I hate writing because it takes so long sometimes. No matter what, I want to figure out how to do this fast."

The "So what?" question can really help to jump start the evening's session. With motivational links made, Brian is often able to really engage and get his work done. But suppose there is no obvious link between assignments and interests. What if some part of a night's homework doesn't feel especially relevant to you or to your child? You can use such assignments as opportunities for your child to deliberately explore how he learns. He can explicitly decide to work on estimating time or finding the best place to study, for example. His "No Matter What's" might be "to find out how long it takes to outline two pages" or "to read in the rocking chair and on the couch to find out where it's easier to concentrate." In this way, your child can find some personal motivation in any assignment, even the most boring or challenging ones.

Some other examples of "No Matter What" might be:

- NMW, I'm going to notice if highlighting helps me read more quickly.

- NMW, I'm going to get half my work done before dinner and notice how that feels.

- NMW, I'm going to work on math until every problem is right.

- NMW, I'm going to read for twenty minutes in the book for my book report.

So now, with the stage set, your child is ready to get to work. "Now what?" is the third question to explore together. This one gets into the how of the night's assignments:

- How are you going to do this assignment?

- What will help you remember what you learn tonight?

- How could you make this assignment fun?

Since learning really is at the heart of homework, I think there's little point in doing it unless you can make the learning stick. We remember what we learn most readily when it is fun, when it involves us, excites us, engages us in all of our senses. To be honest, it's not every night that I feel like I have the time or the imagination to make homework fun, but I believe it is one of the most time- and energy-efficient uses of my brainpower. And it doesn't have to be difficult or complicated. We are so used to thinking about homework as a chore, as something we need to make our children do. What if it really were fun?

Think back to an experience in your education that has stayed with you, one that you will never forget. Which of your senses were involved? Which were left out, if any? One such experience for me was a field trip to the Heinz pickle factory when I was in second grade. This was a truly unforgettable time. More than forty years later, in my mind, I can still see the huge steel beams above us in the enormous, echo-y warehouse-like rooms with the gigantic shiny machinery. Mostly, I remember the smell—it was like being *in* a jar of pickles. We were told the story of how the little cucumbers become pickles; we watched them swimming in their brine. We got little pickle pins and free samples. I couldn't wait to tell my family all about it. All of my senses were involved.

Now, also think of an experience in your schooling from which you remember very little. I think about a high school literature class in which we read a series of novels and discussed them in class. I tried to be invisible in this class. I was not interested in the novels and actually read very few of them. I remember purchasing a set of Cliff Notes that helped me pass the tests. I still get a twinge of guilt when I see copies of *A Mill on the Floss*. Very little of me was invited into this English class or into the homework assignments that related to it.

Many of the tasks our kids bring home have the feel of the latter example. That's what makes homework drudgery, a chore. But it doesn't have to be that way. While it's not possible to plan a field trip for every subject every night, it is important to keep the multisensory effectiveness of field trips alive and well in your thinking about daily homework sessions.

What is the mix of sensory input and output that works the best for your child? Let's reflect again on your child's favorite teachers:

- How did they teach? How did they make learning fun?

- How was your child challenged in new ways?

- What new or different aspects of your child got included in learning?

Kinesthetic—expanding ways to involve body, hands, or emotions

Visual—expanding ways to see or create in writing or with artwork

Auditory—expanding ways to listen or express in words, music, sound

What kinds of changes have made the difference in how your child has responded to various subjects? It may not be just the content, but also how each subject has been taught. Kids respond very differently to different kinds of teaching approaches. For example, Natalie is delighted that her science teacher this year offers new experiments every week; she loves using her hands to learn; she loves trying things out. Scott, on the other hand, gets lost and frustrated doing hands-on activities, so he did better last year with a textbook-and-discussion approach to science.

Caitlin is a child who learned to read on her own before she started school. So, even though she loves to read and spends lots of her free time devouring books, she wouldn't ever say that reading is her favorite subject. How it is taught in school bores her. Caitlin loves her social studies teacher this year because he really gets the kids involved in many ways. Each unit begins with reading historical fiction, which delights Caitlin. This is followed by discussions and research, culminating in an experiential "Day of the Decade" with plays, games, food, art, and costumes to make each time period come alive. Suzanne, Caitlin's best friend, struggles with reading, so she was not thrilled with social studies this year until the first "Day of the Decade" came along. She now gets motivated to do the research necessary to really take part in the culminating experience that brings all of the learning together for her.

Evan is a student who also loves reading and writing, but when his language arts teacher this year required verbal memorization and spelling bees, he did terribly. He could write the words correctly, but had great difficulty spelling verbally.

Bring to mind your child's natural interests for a moment. Is there a certain approach being used that matches how your child has always loved to learn? Jeremy's mom told me that he related to the world by asking endless juicy questions, even as a toddler. It was no surprise to me, then, that he got excited any time we had class discussions, or small-group work where he really had time to express his views and ask his questions. He has since felt totally stifled in classes where he was required to be quiet most of the time. On the other hand, Winston goes crazy in classes where there's mostly talk. He loves art, especially sculpture and photography, where he can make beautiful things with his hands. Too much talking seems to get in the way of his learning and creating. Brian responded really well to his kindergarten teacher, who played the guitar and taught many concepts through songs. Her teaching style was a good match for his love of music. What patterns like these do you notice for your child?

In reading the lists below, think about where your child's most and least favorite interests and skills would fit. What perceptual channels—auditory, visual, or kinesthetic—does your child use most readily, both when learning and when expressing herself, either on her own or at school? This can give you clues about the approaches that might enliven her homework sessions most easily.

Visual Expressive	Auditory Expressive	Kinesthetic Expressive
(to create what can be seen)	*(to create what can be heard)*	*(to create w/hands and bodies, move, do, express emotions)*
Drawing/coloring	Reciting a poem	Acting out a story
Painting	Answering a question	Doing a science experiment
Planning a garden	Giving an oral report	Building a model
Making eye contact	Making up a rhyme	Shooting baskets
Choosing hairstyle, jewelry	Having a spelling bee	Running a relay
Picking a color scheme	Making sound effects	Sharpening a pencil
Showing someone your room	Talking to a friend	Playing soccer
Doing a worksheet	Singing	Jiggling
Practicing handwriting	Telling a joke	Typing
Decorating a bulletin board	Asking for help	Walking
Writing a story	Discussing a topic	Washing dishes
Making a chart	Yodeling	Laughing/crying
Taking notes	Making a speech	Fixing a faucet
Diagramming sentences	Telling someone what to do	Working out at the gym

Visual Receptive	Auditory Receptive	Kinesthetic Receptive
(to see, observe, watch, look)	*(to listen, hear)*	*(to touch, sense, taste, smell, feel emotions)*
Reading a book	Listening to music	Tasting a strawberry
Watching a play	Hearing a lecture	Touching a model of something
Observing a science experiment	Eavesdropping on a conversation	Pursuing what's interesting
Seeing a movie	Hearing Noise in the hall	Feeling the rain on your face
Looking at magazines	Listening to a tape	Soaking in the bathtub
Watching a demonstration	Hearing someone's opinion	Being touched
Watching TV	Listening to an oral report	Comparing weights or textures
Looking in the mirror	Hearing the sounds of nature	Feeling amused
Looking out the window	Listening to instructions	Getting a drink of water
Reading from the chalkboard	Noticing someone's tone of voice	Smelling lunch
Observing people at the mall	Hearing someone call your name	Holding a pet or wild animal
Stargazing	Picking up your voice mail	Sleeping

It may be difficult to separate these aspects of our senses. Many of our everyday activities use a mix of these channels, combinations of our senses. In fact, you may find that your child uses all of them in his favorite activities. Playing the piano certainly creates sound (auditory expressive), but it uses our fingers to do so (kinesthetic expressive). If we are reading music, we are also visually receptive, and we are usually hearing and feeling what we play as well (auditory and kinesthetic receptive). Two people may engage in the same activity but emphasize the use of different channels in doing it. Take painting, for example. One person may love to paint in order to create things that are visually beautiful. For someone else, the product may be secondary to the opportunity to use her body in an active way or to express a feeling in color.

Although we all use each of these channels both to receive information and to express ourselves, one of the ways we are different is that we have very different relationships, degrees of comfort, and levels of experience with these channels. We all tend to use some much more often than others. We may have had more experience singing and playing music than we have with drawing and painting. We may be more comfortable being physically active than talking in a group, or vice versa. Some of us may love to dance in our living rooms or sing in the shower but would never consider entering a dance contest or being a soloist in the choir. With some of these sensory "tools," we may love to be receptive but be hesitant to express ourselves—we might love to go to art museums, but would feel shy trying to sculpt on our own. With another channel just the opposite may be true—we may love to express ourselves physically (sports could be our favorite pastime), but we may feel far away from our emotions, one receptive side of kinesthetic.

These details about your child's natural choices are very important clues about how your child learns most comfortably. Going with the grain of your child's mind involves, first of all, using the channels he has the most fun with as the place to start in enlivening homework sessions. *Play is the most effective learning tool.* Using movement or music or color can help make even the dullest assignments less boring. Making sure that all of your child's senses are involved, even the ones he hesitates to use on his own, will fully engage your child's mind and help make learning stick.

How can you invite your child to be receptive and expressive in auditory, visual, and kinesthetic ways when doing homework? Here are some suggestions for you to try together, organized by channel.

Kinesthetic options are most often left out when we think about doing homework. For all learners, omitting kinesthetic expression makes learning incomplete. Including it can enliven whatever we do. By engaging your child in the activities that follow, you can add the missing kinesthetic piece.

Relate the subject to past experience, either physically or emotionally:

- Make a list of all the verbs that describe things you've done since you got up this morning.

- Remember how you felt when the bullies approached you on the playground? What were your choices? How might the Native Americans have had similar feelings when the explorers arrived? What were their choices?

- If our cat weighs ten pounds, how many cats would it take to weigh as much as that elephant?

- What rides at the carnival use centrifugal force?

- When have you felt left out like the character in the story?

Embody the concept. Act out the story. Physically become what you are studying:

- Become a raindrop in the water cycle.

- Move like Jupiter does around the Sun.

- Stand where the nine would be in 900.

- Make faces to express the feelings of the main characters.

- Create equilateral, isosceles, and scalene triangles with your arms, a ruler, and the floor.

Find or make a model. Use manipulatives:

- Create the parts of the circulatory system with baggies, rubber bands, a sponge, and yarn. What else could you use?

- Use marbles to find all the factors of twelve or twenty-four or ninety-six.

- Practice spelling words with magnetic letters.

- Use Lego people to re-enact the Battle of Lexington and Concord.

- Make flash cards with phonics patterns. Sort them by sound.

Touch an example. Collect samples:

- Find rocks that are metamorphic, igneous, and sedimentary.

- Dissect a flower to study its parts.

- Collect objects whose names you know in French and put them in piles by gender.

- Find all the objects in your house that conduct static electricity.

- Gather food products from your kitchen that have at least four grams of fat per serving.

Use taste and smell:

- Prepare foods or go to restaurants that serve food from the countries you are studying. (Spain, Portugal, Ethiopia, Korea, Vietnam, France, Thailand, etc.)

- Go to medieval festivals or simulated historical sites. Partake of the victuals. Make note of the aromas. (Don't forget the stables, the blacksmith shop, and the bakery.)

- Read the *Smelly Old History Book* series by Mary Dobson, including *Tudor Odors* and *Roman Aromas*. These are books that come with smells!

- Find and smell the spices the explorers were traveling to find.

- Discover the areas for sweet, sour, bitter, and salty flavors on your tongue.

- Practice spelling words with pretzel sticks or shoestring licorice. When you've learned the words, eat them.

Too often, visual options involve just reading books with small margins and tiny print, or poor photocopies with unclear pictures. Our kids are asked to read and take notes and write the answers to questions. But there are more fun and easy ways to engage kids visually as well.

Find nonlinear ways to take notes or collect thoughts:

- Make a wall chart of World War I battles out of "Post-its.™"

- Create a time line showing the sequence of events in *Romeo and Juliet*, with spokes on each event indicating the characters involved.

- Make a web to gather ideas for creative writing.

- Choose simple symbols for American states or countries in Europe. Group them by region or by alliances during World War II.

Make visuals:

- Create a list of favorite adjectives or adverbs to choose from in creative writing. This could be a collage of magazine pictures.

- Make a chart showing "families" of words, and "outlaws," those that don't belong to any family.

- Draw a diagram showing the relationships between protons, electrons, and neutrons.

- Make webs of 1-12 and all of the factors of each.

- Draw outlines of the shapes of spelling words and then fill them in with the letters.

Make images in your mind:

- Make a movie in your mind of Marie Antoinette and the French Revolution.

- Study for a test on literature by going through the events of the story as though you are looking at old snapshots in your mind.

- Do a division problem perfectly, watching it step-by-step in your mind.

Find photos of the real thing:

- Collect photos of famous people you are reading about.

- Find pictures of things made from petroleum products.

See the real thing:

- Watch squirrels in the park long enough to see them eat or store food.

- Get a cow's eye from a butcher shop and dissect it to see the actual parts of the eye.

- Go to a performance of *Beowulf* after you have read it.

- Visit an important historical site in your town.

- Inventory your house for all products made in Japan.

- Take a walk through your home and count how many rectangles, triangles, and circles you see.

Watching movies:

- See *Hamlet* or *Jane Eyre* before reading it in order to know the story line. Then read the play or novel.

- Watch *The Civil War* series to see actual photos of the battles.

- Watch *Chitty Chitty Bang Bang* and compare the book to the movie.

Homework time is usually silent unless your child asks a question. How can we support kids to expand their auditory options so that this vital piece adds to the fun and helps learning stick? It is critical for all learners to hear themselves say what they've learned.

Speaking:

- Play a Jeopardy game with state capitals.

- Become Thomas Jefferson or Harriet Tubman and ask someone to interview you.

- Make up a poem about Cleopatra.

- Pretend to give a radio broadcast from Valley Forge.

- Tell a "Once upon a time story" about a science process such as metamorphosis.

- Explain to someone how to multiply fractions.

Singing and Making Rhythms and Rhymes:

- Practice math facts with the tape *Multiplication Rock*, available from Zephyr Press.

- Make up a song about chemical compounds to the tune of "I've been Working on the Railroad."

- Make up a rap about the respiratory system.

- Make up a commercial for carbohydrates.

Listening:

- Listen to John F. Kennedy's "Ask not . . ." inaugural address.

- Listen to popular Spanish songs and notice how much you can understand.

- Record yourself reciting your vocabulary words and listen to the recording while doing something else.

- Listen to your reading book on tape as you follow along.

Use Sound Effects, Accents:

• Add sound effects to the story you're reading.

• Read your book report in an Australian accent.

When all three channels are used receptively and expressively, learning has a multisensory pathway that will help remembering happen. A rap song to remember the water cycle can be danced and spoken and scribed on large easel paper. Your Jeopardy game with state capitals can include "Post-its™" placed on a large walk-on map on the floor. You can make a diagram of protons, electrons, and neutrons come alive, complete with sound effects. The more ways we can input information, the more ways it can be retrieved when we need it.

Some of these new options will feel like more fun than others to your child. It is probably already clear to you where his "tender places" are, where he is most hesitant to express himself. What kinds of experience does your child consistently avoid? Ironically, these places are often the ones our children most need to complete and solidify their learning. As parents, it's important to help them stretch a little, to gain more experience and develop more comfort in using the channels that feel the most vulnerable, the most unskilled. Here are some examples from the classroom that show how learning playfully can help our children in those areas where they feel the least confident.

Crystal had great fun becoming a character in a story, acting it out and explaining what happened. But putting her story in writing or answering written questions about it was always the hard part for her. It helped her to walk around and tape-record her story; then she could transcribe it from the tape, at her own pace.

Winston loved using his hands; he created a wonderfully detailed model of the solar system, but he could not easily remember the names of any of the planets. I had him make a masking tape replica of the orbits on the floor. Then he walked through each one, repeating a rhyme we had created as a class.

Robin was a very good student. She loved to think and talk and ask questions about sophisticated concepts. Helping Robin get her learning "in her bones" was really important. Periodically, she would prepare and present little playlets, becoming the characters in the story we had read or a famous person in history she admired.

Jeremy could talk a blue streak, but he felt really challenged by tests and most written work. He got flustered because his thoughts always came faster than he could get them down on paper. It seemed to help him to study for tests and write first drafts standing up, using markers on an easel. Using his whole body helped slow his thoughts down. When he found a way to study that involved writing, it helped him do better on written tests.

Saundra could create masterful projects on her own with little or no verbal support, but she had trouble explaining what she had done or what she had learned. What worked for her was to picture in her mind the steps she took in doing her project and to talk her way through what she saw.

Brady almost always found the usual school stuff very easy, especially reading and writing. To deepen his learning, I would ask him questions about how what we were studying related to his life. I sometimes planned simple projects for him, for those days when I knew he would finish his written work early.

Together with your child, increase your awareness of the kinds of fun options that enhance her child's involvement and learning. As this process unfolds, try different things at different times. Your child may need different enhancements for math than for social studies or art.

This is not just one more place to "do for" your child. The point here is to expand the repertoire of personally effective ways in which your child can approach a learning task. Before long, she will know what she needs and will be more able to ask for it both at school and at home. This is what we are aiming for, kids who know their own minds and can advocate for themselves. If Rosie knows she needs to say aloud what she knows, she may ask the teacher for permission to talk to a study buddy for two minutes between stating important points. If Joshua knows he can listen better if he can move, he may ask to stand in the back of the class.

I hear some of you saying, "Oh, puleeez! This is too much! I can't possibly help my child with this kind of intensity every night. Too many subjects, too little time!" You're right! You *can't* do this every night with every assignment. This is something to explore over time with your child. Remember that this is not just about making homework fun. You are helping your children learn how to approach any task with engagement and aliveness, how to put all of themselves—mind, body and spirit—into everything they do.

Reflection

* What have you learned about how to fully engage your children in their learning?

* What has been the effect of "What?" "So What?" and "Now What?" on your homework sessions?

> *"Someone who has completely lost his way in the forest, but strives with uncommon energy to get out of it in whatever direction, sometimes discovers a new unknown way: this is how geniuses come into being— who are then praised for their originality."*
>
> —FRIEDRICH NIETZSCHE

CHAPTER 7

Understanding Concentration, Confusion, and Distraction: Managing Movements of the Mind

Your child's learning is reflected on her math worksheet or in the science project she creates, but learning doesn't all happen there. Much of it happens in the mind. When we are learning, the mind must pay attention to itself. When we witness confusion and distraction, we have called it *inattention,* even "attention deficit"; but what we are really witnessing is our children's minds turning their attention inward. In order for new information to get fully digested, it must be chewed and swallowed, churned and sorted, stored and dispersed. This is what's happening in our minds, beneath the surface, when we experience confusion and distraction.

So, let's give these behaviors new names. We need to honor the processes that they signal; we need to give them credit for what they do for us. In concentration, confusion, and distraction, what we are witnessing is really three different kinds of attention: *focused, exploratory,* and *expanded attention.* Each of these kinds of attention is necessary for our minds to learn something thoroughly, for us to make new knowing our own.

Before we go any farther, I want you to take a rest stop and think about your child. This time, though, I want you to think about her when she's not doing homework. Let your mind take you to moments that delight and puzzle you in your lives together. Select one set of answers for each category:

Focused attention (concentration):

When does your child get energized and alert? When can she stay with something for a long time?

- When going for a walk, playing sports, getting a backrub, eating a snack, building something?

- When talking, singing, listening to the radio, playing music?

- When writing, drawing, cleaning up, watching a movie, reading?

Exploratory attention (confusion):

When does your child seem to be searching for something in his mind, in a way that can be confusing to you? When might he seem indecisive or "fuzzy" in his thinking?

- When in conversation with others? Does he say one thing and mean it but often change his mind? Can he hear both sides of a story easily?

- When he's trying to buy something or do something and looking at all the options? Does he go back and forth between what's real in front of him and a picture in his mind of how he wants things to look?

- When he's in the middle of doing something and it doesn't feel right to him? Does he often feel torn, have conflicting feelings at the same time?

Expanded attention (distraction):

When does your child get daydreamy, "spaced out" or "lost in thought"?

- When reading? when drawing or doodling? when watching the sunset? when watching TV or a movie?

- When playing outside? when doing something with her hands? when she's touched? when she's petting the cat?

- When listening to a conversation or lecture? when listening to music? when answering a question?

In taking this rest stop, I hope you have found moments you really appreciate with your child, ones when you think she is using her mind well, when she's totally engaged with or deeply considering something that's important to her. This is what's trying to happen when our kids get confused and distracted doing homework. But it's as though these behaviors have been written in an unfamiliar, foreign language. Until now, we have been unable to decode their meaning accurately.

People have learned to love sharks and wolves by getting close enough to these awesome creatures to notice their habits, by being willing to watch what they do through the "eyes of their hearts." You might think of confusion and distraction as the wolves and the sharks of the homework process. Almost fifteen years ago, Dawna helped me to let go of my frustration with my own mind long enough to notice what was really happening there, as if I were a loving and curious wildlife scientist. She has given me a wondrous gift of understanding which I gladly begin to pass on to you.

It's not difficult to recognize our kids' confusion or distraction, but it seems quite challenging to let go of the old interpretations we have of these behaviors. When I'm teaching now or helping Brian with homework and I see that familiar glazed look, it's still hard not to think I've lost him, or that he's just wasting time. Everything I had been taught about learning led me to believe that if my kids weren't alert and enthusiastic, they weren't ready to learn, in fact, they weren't even able to learn.

Paying attention, concentration, staying on task—these are all terms we use for what we think we are aiming for in learning. As a teacher, having all of my kids "with me" was a goal that I strived for in every activity, with every lesson.

I fall into the same trap sometimes with Brian, when he's doing homework. I want him to not let himself get distracted, to not fall prey to confusion. I want him to just "get it done."

What I have come to understand is that learning is a dynamic process. Our minds won't stay still; they must move. In the approach to learning I have studied with Dawna, we now use the image of a spiral to help us understand this movement. If we follow this image along its pathway from the beginning point to its widest arc and back again, the continuous flow reflects the movement of our minds from focused attention, through exploratory attention, to expanded attention and then back. The mind expands and contracts like a spiral, as we think, learn, and process what we know.

Let's explore an example now that will help you grasp what is happening as the mind moves through these three kinds of attention. Remember the spiral as you read the following story. Imagine that Jeremy is in Mr. Watson's science class, which is studying the ecosystems of ponds. Mr. Watson begins by asking a question about ponds, introducing the topic for the day. Jeremy is right there with him, at the point of his spiral, very alert. His hand is raised; he's ready to define ponds, to tell Mr. Watson all the facts he knows: the size dimensions that differentiate a pond from a lake, the varieties of living things that make ponds their homes, and more. Jeremy is bringing focused attention to this moment. He's concentrating well and Mr. Watson is confident that Jeremy is "getting" what he's been trying to teach over the last week.

But Jeremy's mind won't stay focused for long. His mind moves, his spiral widens, his thinking changes. He begins to think about the pond he swam in last summer. He remembers the temperature of the water on his skin and he wonders how cold the water in the jar on the counter will be. He is no longer just in the present moment in Mr. Watson's class. His mind is exploring past and present at the same time; it's bringing together what his previous experience has taught him with the new learning of the moment. Mr. Watson calls on Jeremy and he seems confused, not quite "with it" any more. Mr. Watson asks Jeremy to pay attention for just a few more minutes.

But his eyes are drawn to the place on the blackboard where his teacher has written the word "Ponds." Jeremy's mind has moved again, to the widest point of the spiral. His attention is expanded now; his thoughts have moved inward; he's no longer hearing Mr. Watson's voice, but for some reason, he finds himself in the kitchen at home, looking at his mother's bottle of hand lotion on the counter. "Pond's" is on the label. Jeremy's mind has made a connection. He starts wondering if the people who make the hand lotion use ingredients from a pond. Would that be good for your skin? Mr. Watson can tell that Jeremy is no longer with him. He's daydreaming again. So, he announces it's time to choose lab partners and perform some experiments with the pond water.

The spiral of Jeremy's mind contracts now as he becomes aware of the room again and he is thinking about who he would like for a lab partner. He considers Jonathan; he likes his sense of humor, but he knows he could get into trouble with Jonathan. Nathan is too klutzy with lab equipment, he thinks. His mind is using exploratory attention again; he decides on Erica and asks her to join him. He begins to discuss with her the objectives of this lab assignment and he is back at the point of the spiral, concentrating well, in focused attention.

This imaginary classroom scenario could have taken place in a very few minutes. All of what just happened to Jeremy happens for each of us throughout our days, over and over again. In every moment of our waking lives, our minds are expanding and contracting: taking in the world, relating new experience to old, creating new possibilities. We have interpreted confusion and distraction as inattention, when they are important signs of different kinds of attention.

We cannot, we must not, try to stop the movements of our children's minds in the homework process. If we understand what's happening, we can literally "go with the flow" of these movements and enhance the learning that results. We can help our children become aware of and learn to manage the movements of their own minds.

So, what prompts these movements? How can we keep the flow going? In the last chapter, we focused on using all three channels—auditory, visual, and kinesthetic—to engage the entire mind in the learning process. We know that including all of the senses makes both learning and expressing what we've learned more fun, more involving, and more memorable. But why this full engagement is important goes farther than that.

Each of these kinds of stimulation from the world—what we see, what we hear, what we feel and touch—triggers us into a different kind of attention. For each of us, one of our perceptual channels—auditory, visual, or kinesthetic—helps us get focused. A second channel helps us explore. The third channel helps us expand our thinking. We all need all three kinds of stimulation in any learning environment, because this is what helps us move through our entire spiral of attention and helps us digest what we've learned completely.

Let's make this come alive in an example. My son Brian gets very alert and energized when he is listening to music (auditory helps him focus); he gets most confused and most curious when he's using his hands or doing something physical (kinesthetic helps him explore); and he goes deep into his own world when he is reading (visual helps his attention expand).

The way the channels and the kinds of attention link up is not the same for everyone. In my case, visual helps me focus, so when I'm watching TV or reading my mind becomes most alert and outer-directed; auditory helps me explore, so conversations can feel confusing, as I'm aware of both the other person's words and the ones I am hearing in my mind at almost the same time; kinesthetic helps me reach expanded thinking, so I can feel daydreamy in the midst of almost any kind of physical activity.

This link-up between the kinds of sensory stimuli and the different kinds of attention helps us to understand some of the ways we are different as learners. Some of us, like Brady, need to see something in order to get focused. But the same visual input—a chart or a diagram—that helps Brady concentrate, takes Crystal into expanded attention; she gets lost in thought when given something to look at. Jeremy needs to hear something in order to get focused and ready to learn. But Saundra is overwhelmed and spaced out by too many words. Kids like Winston need their hands or bodies involved in order to concentrate. But the kinds of physical activity that might help Winston focus also triggers Robin into spacy, expanded attention.

This new information has helped me to understand what was happening to the kids in my classroom and why with one kind of input I always got three different responses. A specific stimulus, perhaps a discussion question, triggered Jeremy and Robin into alert, focused attention; it caused Brady and Crystal to compare and contrast what was being said with other words in their memories as it triggered exploratory thinking; and this same question took both Winston and Saundra on extended daydreams as expanded thinking made associations between the words of the present and things they'd heard long ago.

What I realize now is that the kind of input I was offering my kids is what affected their attention. If I used only one kind of teaching method, with only one kind of sensory stimulation, I kept some kids alert and focused, but other kids would be consistently distracted or confused. If I used a variety of methods, not only was it more fun, but I was triggering all three kinds of attention in everyone, inviting them to use their whole minds to learn the subject matter thoroughly.

One important way you can be supportive as a homework coach is to learn to recognize the different kinds of attention and what triggers them in your children. You can help them anticipate how different assignments will affect them and help them manage the movements of their mind no matter what. Let's spend a little time getting more familiar with each of these kinds of attention.

Recognizing Concentration— Focused Attention

I think of concentration as the ability to attend to something exclusively for a period of time. There is a kind of hungry, excited energy, a sense of fun, enjoyment, and easy satisfaction when we are concentrating. Our mind is focused and we can keep doing the same thing without wavering. While concentrating, my mind feels like a laser beam, shutting out all but one set of thoughts, images, or processes. This period of time, no matter how long or short, might be referred to as someone's attention span.

We think of some people as being better at focusing than others. I believe we are all capable of concentration; what varies is the activity to which we are able to give this kind of attention. When Brian was small, I remember being amazed at how long he could spend listening to songs and singing the words. In contrast, he had almost no ability to concentrate in a museum. His eyes could not stay focused on one picture for more than a few seconds. Brian has a long attention span when he is listening, but when he has to look at something, his attention span is very short; he cannot concentrate for very long at all.

I was asked to observe a fifth-grader whose parents had been told had attention-deficit disorder. This child could not bring himself to alert and focused attention when asked a question or when others were talking as he was trying to work because auditory stimuli distracted him. However, when he went to gym class, he was able to concentrate for long periods of time with a kinesthetic task; in fact, his attention span was far longer than most of his non-ADD classmates.

I remember taking some kids to the Discovery Zone, one of those indoor playground centers, and feeling very "spaced out" by all of the physical activity around me, since kinesthetic input triggers expanded attention for me. I remember unconsciously reading all of the signs, menus, and notices I could find, trying to visually stimulate myself back into focused attention.

Consider these questions about your child. They can help you begin to determine which channel helps your child get focused.

What's the best way to get your child's attention when you need it?

- Speak loudly enough so he can hear you

- Stand in front of him so he can see you

- Touch him so he'll notice you

How does your child learn most quickly? How does she think "fast"?

- By talking or asking questions

- By reading, watching, writing, or drawing

- By using her hands or her whole body

What's the easiest way for your child to greet someone he doesn't know? How does he like to get to know them?

- By shaking hands, by doing something together

- By saying hello, by having a conversation

- By making eye contact, by seeing their home, their things

What kinds of details does your child remember most easily? What is he most "picky" about?

- How things look

- How things are said

- How things are done, how things feel

What is going on in the mind when we are concentrating? We are receiving lots of data from the world and trying to make sense of it. We are noticing details, organizing them, quickly finding a familiar context in which to put what we are taking in. "Oh, this story is about a girl my age." "This experiment is about magnets." "This song sounds like Beethoven." This part of our mind keeps track of what's familiar and establishes routines that can help us feel safe in new experiences. It loves to create structure and organization. This part of our mind helps create order out of chaos.

When concentrating, we can learn and remember details quickly. This is the part of our mind that can cram for a test. It thinks fast. It can take something in and spit it right back out in the form in which it was received —like a copy machine, a robot, a tape recorder. It is the part of our mind seeking the one right answer, the simple solution. This is where we process information quickly. Easy in, easy out.

When we are concentrating, our attention is directed to the outside world. We handle lots of information, but it lies on the surface of our mind. This is the seduction of doing homework in a concentrated fashion. It is simple, it takes the least amount of time and brain power. We are simply using and rearranging someone else's thoughts.

For each kind of learner, there are some assignments that naturally trigger concentration. Kids like Brady are often thought of as good students because it is easy for them to concentrate on visual-auditory tasks typical of school assignments, particularly reading and writing. Saundra and others like her will be naturally triggered into concentration by tasks that require them to see and then do, such as drawing or building.

Robin concentrates best when her assignments call for auditory output, such as oral reports. Studying for tests orally will help her remember what she has learned effectively. Jeremy will also be able to concentrate well when using auditory input and output. Listening to a tape may support him in his studying.

Crystal will be able to concentrate best when an assignment calls for physical activity, such as role-playing or making a model. Winston, too, will be able to stay focused the best when asked to move or to relate to the present learning from past experience.

Many assignments do not trigger concentration naturally for many kinds of learners. Knowing what does help your child focus her attention will help you guide her with suggestions while doing homework. When does your child naturally concentrate? In gym class? How could you incorporate that somehow in a night's studying? I heard a wonderful story of a mother whose daughter came in ready to study spelling with her roller blades still on. This girl gets focused kinesthetically and she usually has a terrible time remembering her spelling words. Her mother pulled out the spelling list and they studied together while the girl spun around the kitchen. This study session netted a previously unheard-of 100 percent on the test the next day.

Use what you know about your child to help him concentrate. A favorite rocking chair might help a child who gets alert kinesthetically, like Crystal, read a long passage; its familiar rhythm will trigger her focused attention. Color-code the pieces of a hands-on project to support a child who gets energized visually. Learners like Robin who focus auditorily can talk aloud to themselves or to a partner to help them stay with the steps involved in a hands-on science experiment.

The trick is to think about whether the homework assignment will naturally put your child in a focused state of attention. If not, ask yourself what can you add to the assignment—movement, pictures, or sound—to help him become more focused.

Our ability to concentrate is an important resource in the learning process. But it is not the whole story. If what we study uses only this part of our minds, we are depriving the world and ourselves of the deeper creative ideas that arise from expanded thinking. When we allow the rest of our mind to come into play, we add more of ourselves to the process and complete learning truly starts to happen. Let's look at the other two kinds of attention and what is happening when we are using them.

Making Time for Confusion— Exploratory Attention

You know the look: the scrunched-up face, the little whiny voice that says, "I don't get it," the shoulders raised in a semi-permanent shrug. I used to think this was a sure sign of failure, my failure as a teacher and a parent. "Do I have to start all over again?" "How can I help you understand?"

Think about your child with these questions. They can help you sort out which channel triggers confusion and exploratory attention in your child:

How does your child naturally like to explore?

- Saying the same thing in many different ways

- Experimenting with how things look—furniture arrangements, hairstyles, clothes, handwriting

- Making up new ways to play old games

What helps your child make decisions?

- Talking things out

- Seeing the options available

- Trying activities to notice how they feel

Which of these skills tends to be inconsistent for your child?

- How she expresses herself verbally

- How she performs physically

- How she writes or draws

What's happening when we experience confusion? At this stage of mental metabolism, information has gone in deep enough to churn around with what we already know. Our attention alternates between our inner world and the outer one, between our memories and our present experience. Our old learning structures are being integrated with the new ones. As our sense of what we thought we knew begins to break down, even slightly, we experience what's called confusion. We are sorting what is coming in. We are in "seesaw" mind, going back and forth between what could be and what was. We are exploring ways of thinking, trying on options, sorting possibilities. We are in process, jarred out of complacency by new information but not yet ready to express ourselves with it. If we keep trying to express from this place, our confusion becomes apparent to others. We waffle, we can't make up our minds. We hem and haw, we sit on the fence. We change our mind.

What our mind needs here is the time to explore, the luxury of getting curious. We need to try several ways to say things, to do things, to see things. We need to plunge deeper into the issues at hand, to compare the old way with the new directly, to cogitate, to consider.

How often do we let ourselves explore in this way? How often do we allow our children to do this? In our hurry-up world, we are expected to get off the fence immediately, get on with our lives right now, make split-second decisions. But this goes against the grain of our minds. We function most effectively when we pause and reflect on our actions, take time to make up our own minds.

Consider this example. Brady was stymied by his essay assignment. He had to take a clear stand on whether Christopher Columbus should still be honored as the discoverer of the New World or whether he should be admonished in the history books as the person who began the destruction of the native cultures in the western hemisphere. Brady sat in front of the word processor for several hours trying to peck out sentences that made some sense. His writing was confusing to read. So his father encouraged him to talk about what he was writing. It became clear to Brady's dad that his son could hear both sides of the story and was having trouble committing to one. He was caught between what he had always been taught about Columbus and the new multicultural perspective he was considering. He needed time to sort out what he believed. Brady was really helped by having a sounding board. He needed to verbalize his confusion and talk through both opinions. Taking the time to explore saved Brady time in the long run. The writing was easy after his thoughts had been spoken and clarified.

Brady's father could have simply fed him the thoughts that justified one viewpoint in order to help him get the assignment finished. It's common for parents to have that impulse. When our child is confused, we may just jump in with the answer: x = 36; Ohio; *Catcher in the Rye*. But when we solve the confusion by providing the answer, we stop the learning process. Instead, when your child is confused, encourage him to slow down the process, just as Brady's father did. Ask your child to become aware of the differences between the new and the old. Ask him to go back to what he already knows and consider where the new information is asking him to stretch:

"Yesterday all of the subtraction problems had bigger numbers on the top than on the bottom and today sometimes I have to subtract from numbers with a zero."

"I understand the words in this poem, but the teacher wants us to write about what the poet's symbols mean."

"I just read that the U.S. had internment camps for Japanese people during World War II. I thought the Nazis were the only ones who rounded people up."

Rather than providing the answer, support your child to explore by asking further questions, by trying new approaches to the stuck place, by mapping possible routes between here and there:

"Use these chips to show me how you did the problems yesterday. What pile can you borrow chips from in the problems today?"

"What is a symbol, anyway? How do you use symbols when you talk and write? What's one word in this poem that is really a symbol?"

"What feelings might the Nazis and the U.S. government have had in common that would have prompted them to respond by setting up camps? When have you had those feelings?"

Certain kinds of assignments will trigger confusion for different kinds of learners. A multiple-choice test might cause some kids to sort. All the answers may look right to them and they need time to explore and eliminate. A simple discussion question may cause confusion in another child; she may need to talk her way through several answers before deciding which one sounds right.

A straightforward science experiment may send some kids into explore mode; they may want to try out many ways they think the process could be done.

Because we call this aspect of learning "confusion," exploratory attention is given the least amount of space and airtime in most schools. Be willing to indulge the curiosity underneath the confusion, even just a little, and your child's learning will be more effective, and he or she will be more content with the outcome.

Valuing Distraction—Expanded Attention

When our children get distracted, we imagine that the learning process has stopped entirely. Just because it *seems* that nothing is going in, that doesn't mean that nothing is going on. When your child feels unavailable to you, when he is spaced out, dreamy, glazed over, gone away, a vital part of the learning process may be taking place. Often below the surface of consciousness, with our attention turned inward, the mind is synthesizing new information with all of the already-stored life experiences in our long-term memory banks. It is making connections between tidbits of memory and incoming data so that what can emerge are unique creations and new ways of thinking.

Explore your child's trigger to expanded attention with these questions.

What can most easily distract your child from the task at hand? What makes her get "spacy"? What seems to overwhelm her most quickly?

- Sounds, voices, noises, music

- Pictures, the view, faces, eye contact

- Touch, feelings, sensations, activity

What kinds of activities does your child feel shy about doing in public, but like to do when she's on her own?

- Free-form movement, such as dancing, biking, swimming, swinging

- Singing, humming, wordplay, imitations, storytelling

- Doodling, painting, writing, drawing

What does your child have the hardest time remembering?

- How things look,, peoples' faces

- How to pronounce words, what people said

- How she felt, what she did

Which channel do you think triggers your child into expanded attention?

It may be hard to appreciate this state of mind without being reminded of the delightful surprises that can come out of it. I remember one little girl, Tina, who explained that one moment she was looking at her math paper, and the next she was on her grandmother's front porch. As things turned out, the number Tina was asked to add was also the number of her grandmother's street address. Working on this deep synthesizing level, her mind had made a mental connection.

We've all had moments when we've gotten frustrated with a problem we're trying to solve, so we go and do something else, only to find that the solution pops into mind, seemingly out of nowhere. In these moments, we've allowed distraction to do its best work. We've allowed our minds to ponder deeply, to take a rest from figuring things out, and in expanded attention, associations are made, new possibilities are born.

As the story is told, Charles Darwin was riding on the top of a two-decker London bus when some of the key points of the theory of evolution emerged in his mind. There was nothing necessarily magical about that bus; it was his mind that was magical. He was using it well, allowing his mind take all he had been thinking and weave it together in a profoundly unique way.

The channel that triggers expanded attention for your child contains the most generative power of the mind. It's so ironic that the part of ourselves we feel most hesitant to use, the part that can frustrate us the most when misunderstood, is the part that, when well used, is the most creative. Einstein's thoughts have changed how we think of the universe, yet he didn't learn to speak until age seven, when his mother taught him to sing. Picasso's unique way of seeing and painting the world blossomed from a visual channel that stubbornly resisted learning to read and write. Eleanor Roosevelt's great feeling for humankind flourished even though she was a kinesthetically shy and awkward child.

How can we as parents begin to embrace this "lost in thought" part of our child's mind as the "tender place" that needs the most nurturance? How can we retrain ourselves to support our children to take time to think deeply, when it appears that they are not thinking at all?

There are some kinds of assignments that naturally call for expanded attention. This kind of thinking, designed for brainstorming, for generating new possibilities and patterns, is called for in creative writing or the design of a science project. Listening to favorite instrumental music or humming may get the creative juices flowing for kids who get triggered into expanded attention auditorily. Doodling may help learners go to this state of wonder with visual stimulation. Meandering around the room or outdoors might get those minds triggered kinesthetically into this expanded attention. It may be hard sometimes for some kids to relax into this state of mind when so much schooling involves reshaping others' ideas. Give this time. Practice often. Notice how few minutes it takes for your child to feel refreshed and newly motivated.

When your child can't stay with the task at hand, his mind

may be calling for time-out to process things more deeply. His mental cup may be full. This is the time to help your child unwind.

What do we mean by "unwinding?" This is a wonderful word I learned from Dawna that essentially means letting your mind go. Encourage your child to expand her attention in a way that's completely unrelated to subject matter. Suggest that she soak in a bathtub, move to music, go for a walk, or sculpt something in clay. It may be effective for some kids to daydream, doodle, paint, watch a candle flame, or look at the widest view they can find. Others could find a quiet spot to be in silence, listen to the sounds of nature, hum, or play the piano. Do this long enough for relaxation to occur. This nourishes expanded thinking that helps our minds get everything fully integrated.

Be careful not to add more content at this stage. Watching TV or reading comic books is not unwinding. It is adding more to the soup. Songs with words may make the mind more full, while humming or whistling may help it digest what's already there. Doing chores could overload your child. Encourage him just to sit, rock, swing, rest, or pet the cat.

Remember that your child is not being obstinate or lazy when distraction occurs. All three kinds of attention don't come about by magic. They may be evoked, triggered by the kind of input your child is receiving or being asked to use. By managing this input, we change the kind of attention we bring to bear on the problem at hand: focused, exploratory, or expanded. Change channels often to keep the flow going. Understand what's happening when confusion and distraction appear. Expect and welcome those states without getting stuck there. Take confusion into curiosity. Deal positively with distraction. Give your child unwinding time.

When you help your children move through their spiral of attention, you are doing no less than increasing their experience and comfort with their whole minds; you are helping them stretch into their full thinking capacities and creative capabilities.

Reflection

- *What do you know now about what helps your child concentrate?*

- *What have you learned about what confuses him?*

- *How does he like to explore?*

- *What tends to distract your child most easily?*

- *How could you support your child to unwind?*

*"The mind fits the world and shapes it
as a river fits and shapes
its own banks."*

—ANNIE DILLARD

CHAPTER 8

Enhancing Learning Conditions: Personalizing the Study Space

Despite most homework experts' advice, there is no one right way to set up a study space for your child. Many traditional homework guides recommend creating a place devoted exclusively to studying, a place that's quiet, with a desk and chair, good lighting, and few visual distractions. These learning conditions do work well for some people. But there are many variations on the study space theme. In this chapter, you'll get a chance to discover with your child the unique optimal conditions for learning at home. You'll be offered many new options to experiment with in creating a personalized study space. Notice your child's natural choices and discover how some surprising elements might actually enhance her experience of nightly homework sessions.

Take some time to reflect on your child's natural choices.

- In what room does your child usually study? Why do you think he chooses this place?

- How does he make himself physically comfortable?

- Does he sit at a table, study on the bed, spread out on the floor?

- Does he stay in one position or does he move frequently?

- Does your child like to have a snack or drink while studying?

- What seems important to your child about what she sees or doesn't see in her study environment?

- What helps her to produce work that looks good?

- Does your child prefer silence, noise, or music when he studies? Does this vary? Why do you think it changes?

- What else is characteristic of your child's study habits?

- How are these habits like those of your child when he's working on a hobby or other interest?

The sights, sounds, and physical conditions around your child when she studies are moving her mind through the thinking spiral, for better or worse. Whatever your child sees, hears, and feels in your home can be helping her or, in some cases, keeping her from getting her homework done. Our kids' natural choices are often good ones for them, whether it's spreading out on the floor, listening to music, or staring out the window for a few minutes, even though those same choices may not be good ones for us.

I realized recently that I had been having an ongoing unspoken disagreement with Brian about the light in his room when he studies. The nightly scenario went something like a comedy routine. He would turn on the overhead light when he first walked into his room and every time I came by I would I turn out the overhead and turn on a brighter, more direct light. The indirect light from the ceiling seemed so dim to me, I couldn't imagine he was choosing to study that way. It finally occurred to me that I was trying to get Brian to use the kind of light I need when I study. We began talking about his use of the overhead light and some of the other choices that he makes: to work on his lap, to have the TV on at times, to spread out on the floor in the living room when he writes. I realized my preferences had been getting in the way of our discovering together what really worked for Brian.

In the classroom, too, it's clear that different students need very different conditions to learn well. Winston was a child who fascinated me, because he also frequently made choices that went against the grain of *my* mind. I work best sitting in one place, with little or no clutter on my desk. I was constantly telling Winston to sit down, or to put his toys or extra pencils out of sight and out of reach. One day I realized that Winston got the most work done as we were easing into snack time, when it was okay to move around, when it was okay to be holding something in his hands, when he was eating and drinking. I had assumed that all of these choices were distractions for Winston, that they had been taking him away from doing his work. In fact, many of these options helped him stay on task. So, I began making some allowances for Winston to spread out on the floor, to do his work standing up at his desk, or to have something small in his hands.

Although Winston needed movement, he easily got distracted by noise of any kind. I couldn't put him anywhere near Robin, who seemed to need to mumble to herself while reading. Robin could easily sit still to study, but Winston's moving and jiggling drove her crazy. So, I set up a carrel in one corner of the room for Robin, where her voice wouldn't disturb Winston and where she wouldn't get distracted by his moving around.

Because we are triggered in different ways by various stimuli, some elements in the study space will help your child concentrate; others will help if he needs to brainstorm, if he needs to sort something out, or if he needs to create something. Remember that your child needs all three channels to trigger the entire learning process when he's studying, both in the classroom and at home. If an assignment itself doesn't call for auditory, visual, and kinesthetic elements specifically, and if you don't have the time and energy to help your child add them, they can be provided by the environment in more general ways. Our home environments provide lots of stimulation. It's a matter of choosing the kind of stimulation that will fill in the missing pieces or augment the perceptual stimuli of the learning assignment itself.

I've come to understand Brian's need for background noise. He gets focused most easily when he's hearing something. But many of his homework assignments require him to read and to write, both of which involve his expanded visual channel. If we don't have time to discuss what he is learning on a given night, he is still able to concentrate when there is other sound in the room; the sound actually helps him concentrate more effectively than silence would. Other kids will find other options more helpful. Justin used to space out for hours when given long reading assignments. He has found that simply being in the living room with his parents, if they are reading or doing needlework, helps him to stay with his studies more consistently than being alone in his room.

What follows are some questions, organized by perceptual channel, to help you think about your child's home study environment and his or her natural choices within that environment. Each question suggests at least one option that could help your child study effectively; all of these options work well for some learners. Make some new choices together. Experiment and notice what happens.

Be willing to try several options within the same group. Notice which ones are effective and which ones are not. Help your child expand her experience of the many ways she can make learning easy. Sometimes we get stuck because we assume only one option will do the trick. When Valerie's mom realized that kinesthetic input helped her daughter focus, at first she suggested that Valerie squeeze a rubber ball while she read. Valerie actually needed to be much more active kinesthetically to maintain her attention, so she still kept falling asleep over her books. Together, they discovered that peddling on a stationary bike helped Valerie to concentrate while reading.

It's hard to imagine sometimes how little it takes to make a difference in a child's learning experience. Angela discovered that her hand was much more comfortable writing with a fat-barreled pen than a thin No. 2 pencil. This simple change helped her go from a child who rarely did her written assignments to one who approached them more willingly.

Kinesthetic Options:

Does your child like to study alone? Does she work better with companionship? What kind?

- Study buddy: peers doing the same task
- Peer tutor: peers helping her
- Tutor: parent, older sibling, someone you've hired
- Company: others around doing other tasks

Does your child prefer familiar or unfamiliar study spaces? Does your child use one or more of these places to study?

- His bedroom, someone else's bedroom
- Common spaces: living room, dining room, kitchen
- Extra spaces: spare room, study, attic, basement, porch
- Others: bathtub, large closet

Does your child like to study away from home?

- At the library, at another person's home, at school
- While moving: on buses or subways, in the car, on roller blades, while biking, walking
- In public places: at cafes and restaurants
- Outside: in the backyard, in a park, at a picnic table, in a lawn chair, on a blanket

Where does your child choose to sit?

- Chairs with sturdy shapes, meant for one person, for sitting upright
- Soft, pliable furniture, such as armchairs, lounges, beanbag chairs, beach chairs, for more flexible postures
- Couches, beds that can be shared, for spreading out or lying on
- Furniture that moves, such as rocking chairs, swivel chairs, porch swings, chairs on wheels
- Exercise equipment, such as stationary bikes, stairmasters, treadmills
- Floor, with carpet, wood, tile or linoleum

Where does your child choose to write?

- Standard desks and tables to sit at
- Desks built for standing, easels, white boards
- Drafting tables or kitchen bars with tall stools
- Lapboards
- Easel pads on the floor

Does it help your child to eat or drink while studying? Does she chew on pencils or bite her nails? What else could meet this need?

- Snacks, such as pretzels, popcorn, carrots, apples, raisins, protein bars, fruit leather, Cheerios
- Water, milk, juices, energy drinks such as Gatorade, smoothies, protein drinks
- Sugarless chewing gum

Does your child like to study while you cook dinner? Smells may be helping him think. What familiar and pleasant smells might you add?

- Scented candles

- Flowers
- A tissue sprinkled with spices, such as cinnamon, nutmeg, cloves, vanilla, almond, anise
- Air-freshener, potpourri, incense
- Aromatherapy with essential oils
- Cologne

Does your child like to have something to touch while studying? Does your child naturally play with his hair or ears, or pick up small things to handle? How else could this need be met?

- A smooth stone, a piece of clay
- Koosh ball, marbles, Lego pieces
- A soft piece of fabric, an extra pen, a small stuffed animal

Does it help your child to wear the same clothes he wore to school? Does it help your child to change into different clothes?

- Looser, more comfortable clothes, sweats or slippers
- A specific color, a special texture, a kind of warmth
- Clothes with more structure
- A special accessory, such as a hat, belt, scarf, or "reading" glasses that helps your child feel confident

Does your child prefer cooler temperatures to concentrate?

- A window open, a fan on

Does your child need a lot of warmth to feel comfortable?

- Windows closed, an extra blanket, a space heater

Visual Options:

How does visual stimulation affect your child?
Does having something to look at help your child concentrate?

Two-dimensional room decorations

- Posters of favorite people, places, things
- Pictures of family, friends, pets, heroes, heroines
- Abstract images in color or black and white
- Famous paintings
- Artwork of her own
- Words of encouragement—affirmations, poetry, song lyrics, goal statements

Three-dimensional objects

- Visuals in motion—mobiles, pet fish, lava lamp
- Trophies, souvenirs, collections

Would it help your child to change what he sees periodically?
Does your child work better with little or no visual stimulation?

- A blank wall
- Empty picture frames to imagine with

Does your child need natural visual refreshers when she studies?

- View out a window to sunset, sky, trees, neighborhood, yard

What kind of light works best for your child?

- Direct light
- Study lamp on or near desk
- Track lighting
- Movable floor lamp

- Indirect light—overhead light, halogen lamp
- Dim, bright, soft-focus or three-way lights
- White light, yellow light, colored lights, rotating color wheel

How does visual clutter affect your child's studying?

- Does he need his work surface and the area around it to be free of clutter?
- Can she ignore any clutter and still concentrate?

What kinds of supplies help your child produce visually?

Supplies that allow movement

- Large white board with markers
- Easel with pad and markers
- Slate or chalkboard with colored chalk
- Magnetic board and letters

Paper—to brainstorm, practice writing, align numbers and letters

- Easel paper—plain or graph
- Newsprint, large or small
- Lined or unlined paper
- Drawing paper, graph paper, scrap paper
- Construction paper
- Post-it™ notes, index cards

Pens and pencils

- Ball point, roller ball, cartridge ink, felt tip
- Thick point, thin, micro, colors
- Fat barrel, thin barrel
- No. 2, mechanical, drawing

- Erasers, correction fluid
- Ruler, protractor, compass, template
- Word-processor
- Art supplies
- Markers—fine point, thick point, washables, overwriters
- Colored pencils
- Crayons, oil pastels, paints

Auditory Options:

How does sound affect your child while she's studying? Does she concentrate better with sound in the background?
- Radio
- Television
- Household noises—dishwasher, refrigerator
- White noise machines
- Neighborhood sounds

Does she work best with music?
- Filling the room
- Directly in her ear from a headset
- Instrumental with no words—classical, jazz, new age
- Nature sounds on tape
- With words
- Songs that inspire
- Songs that raise her energy level
- Songs that soothe and calm
- Songs in another language

Does your child need complete silence in order to concentrate?

- Closed doors
- Ear plugs
- Headset with no sound

Does your child need to hear what he's reading?

- Listen to story tapes and follow along
- Hear someone read the story as he looks on
- Hear himself read the story out loud
- Listen to his own recorded voice reading the story

Does your child need to produce sound when he studies?

- Read aloud to himself or to you
- Study orally using questions and answers
- Set words to song, rhyme, or rhythm
- Use someone as sounding board to sort thoughts
- Repeat vocabulary or concepts aloud
- Use tape recorder to compose first draft

The learning environment can provide interesting and unusual resources to help your children engage more fully with whatever they are studying. Once you've discovered together what elements support them effectively, they can create the optimal conditions themselves wherever they are on their own. This is a gift that will stand them in good stead as they get older, when they must study and work without your daily support.

Reflection

* What have you discovered about your child's natural study habits?

* What discoveries surprised you?

* What suggestions does your child now have to choose from?

* How could your child use what he's learned on interests other than homework?

"Each mind has its own method."

—RALPH WALDO EMERSON

CHAPTER 9

Getting Stuck and Unstuck: Expanding Mental Resources

It seems that the time we feel most tempted to do homework for our children is when they get stuck. They feel frustrated, we feel frustrated. Many parents worry if they aren't up on the latest math methods or if their own ancient history knowledge feels like ancient history. Sometimes all that's needed is a fresh approach to the subject matter at hand. We can often best support our children by helping them bring the full range of mental resources to their work. When everything grinds to a halt, how can we help them find ways to get the wheels moving again?

Take a few minutes now to reflect on how your child gets stuck and how you both usually cope with it:

- When does your child get stuck?

- Is it usually with one or two subjects? Which ones?

- What perceptual channels are typically being called for?

- Does your child get stuck at about the same time in the evening? How might it be related to energy level?

- How does your child handle getting stuck?

- Does she move on to something else?
- Does she stay with it no matter what?
- Does she take a break and come back to it?
- Does she act out?
- Does she give up?
- Does she ask for help? From you? From others?
- How does she ask for help?
- How do you help most often when your child gets stuck?
- Do you feel that you have to do the work yourself first before you can help?
- Do you try to explain it?
- Do you show him how and then ask him to try again?
- Do you do it with him?
- Do you do it for him?
- What typically is the best approach for both of you?
- How does your child get stuck when pursuing other interests: with art projects, with music lessons, with sports?
- What helps him move through when stuck in those situations?

We each tend to have habitual ways of getting stuck in our minds, familiar places we go to in our thinking and then stay there, spinning around and around. What follows is a brief description of each of the three most popular ways kids get stuck when they are learning, and a list of suggestions for how to support them to get "unstuck." Learners can get stuck while they're too focused, thinking the same things over and over, when they're too expanded, open and vulnerable, or when they get caught in confusion.

The simple guideline that threads its way through all of what follows is: *Change perceptual channels. Help your child rotate among visual, auditory, and kinesthetic approaches to the task at hand.* Obsession often happens one channel at a time. If you can figure out what channel your child is using and help him switch to another, the light at the end of the tunnel often appears. Sometimes all it takes is to shift from being receptive to getting active in the same channel. When your child changes channels, he not only brings another learning tool to the rescue, but he also brings a fresh kind of attention and a new set of thinking skills to the problem. Help your child become aware of when he is stuck. Tell him what you notice and ask him if you can offer suggestions. Help him learn the simple principle of changing channels to get unstuck. This will empower him to solve his own problems, whether you are around or not, and help him develop self-reliance and flexible thinking—two of the most important mental skills for the lifelong learner.

"One-Way Street": Stuck in Focused Attention

Crystal drives her mother crazy, rolling the desk chair back and forth across the kitchen floor. Saundra sweeps every piece of lint off her carpet before she can begin her work. Robin spouts a stream of endless stories, recounting the details of her day to her sometimes-patient father. These kids are stuck in focused thinking, obsessed with details, intent on staying energized, wanting to make contact with their parents, perhaps, rather than dig in to the assignment in front of them.

There are many ways kids get stuck in focused attention. Brady reads cereal boxes and can labels instead of getting started on his math. Jeremy listens to just one more song on his CD, promising himself he'll start his book report soon. Winston changes into three different pairs of sweats, trying to find the right ones for the evening. All the kids are having a hard time getting started. Whether our kids are caught "inhaling" or "exhaling" obsessively, we call this stuckness the "One-Way Street."

In the middle of an assignment, as well, your child can get stuck in a focused way, trying to get details perfect and missing the point of the assignment. With the One-Way Street, we cram for the test, memorize the words, build the project, but don't fully grasp the learning that undergirds it.

Getting unstuck on the "One-Way Street" is usually a matter of going from output to input or from input to output. In supporting your child with an assignment, help her use more than just her focused channel to move the learning beyond short-term into long-term memory. Here are descriptions of One-Way Street and some specific suggestions, organized by channels:

Kinesthetic One-Way Street

- Can't stop moving, touching, eating, seeking comfort

- Can make the model or do the activity, but not get the concept underneath it

- Practices physical skills endlessly

Suggestions:

- Touch your child, help him get comfortable, introduce smell, offer him a drink or snack—encourage him to get receptive kinesthetically.

- Suggest one thing he could start with to get going on his work, perhaps what will be easiest for him to complete.

- Ask him questions, draw diagrams, write down what he says about the activity, so the learning behind it becomes more apparent to him.

- Invite him to use other channels to strengthen his natural skills—suggest he make mental movies of himself doing the activity perfectly, narrating what he sees.

Visual One-Way Street

- Neatens, straightens, cleans up obsessively, looks at everything

- Edits papers word by word, recopies assignments, aiming for visual perfection

- Can read and write without thinking, crams visually for tests without understanding

Suggestions:

- Create a study area that is contained and easily kept in order. Set a time limit on organizing materials.

- Make eye contact with your child or show her something interesting to break into the obsession with cleaning up.

- Encourage your child to draw a picture or write a letter to herself about the night's homework to ease her into it.

- Ask your child to tell you the whole story before she begins writing, to prevent obsession with a perfect first paragraph.

- Ask her to write a first draft by recording and transcribing it.

- Turn off the visual screen on the computer while he writes, so he can edit errors later and not get caught in them as he goes along.

- Talk about how what she's learning relates to her personal experience.

- Encourage your child to find a study partner with whom to review aloud.

- Offer him a drink or snack, rub his back, to ground study time in physical self.

Auditory One-Way Street

- Can't stop talking to self or others, listens compulsively

- Can memorize facts, spit back answers quickly without integrating deeply

- Asks questions and doesn't listen for the answer

Suggestions:

- Put on music without words to get your child receptive in auditory channel.

- Ask your child to describe something that she sees, especially something that is moving, to engage both visual and kinesthetic channels.

- Encourage your child to diagram what she is learning, to understand how the facts are connected.

- Look at text or pictures together. Have your child make a web or map of what he's learning.

- Quiz your child orally, encouraging him to take a breath (time to think) between each question and the answer.

- Have your child write her answers to questions on an easel or white board to engage both her visual and kinesthetic channels.

"In the Mud":
Stuck in Exploratory Attention

Winston whines that he can't decide what to write; his creative writing assignment lies crumpled near the wastebasket. Brady has spent hours struggling with his debate preparation. When he rehearses with his sister, she can't really tell which side he is supporting. Jeremy can't decide whether or not to try out for the school play, and is making himself sick with indecision. All of these kids are stuck "In the Mud." Their minds are sorting options, alternating between different choices endlessly—"maybe this, maybe that." How can you help them?

When we're feeling confused, our exploratory channel needs time to consider many possibilities, but it also needs support to halt the exploration and make a decision. This part of our minds needs to get clear about the criteria for decision-making and then sort the available options accordingly. So much of the torture of "In the Mud" stuckness is that it is often internal and solitary. One of the best ways you can support your child is to help her get the ideas out of her head and into some tangible form. Talk, write, move. Help your child pick one option and test it. Sometimes the options aren't satisfying enough. It could be time to unwind and notice what other choices emerge from the creative, expanded part of the mind. Here are descriptions of "In the Mud" and some specific suggestions, organized by channel:

Kinesthetic In the Mud

- Gets overwhelmed with contradictory feelings, not knowing which way to move, what to do for a project, where to begin on the night's work

- Tries things out, dabbles, sometimes all or none of the options feels right

- Gets confused by others' feelings, needs to notice own feelings

Suggestions:

- Encourage your child to get physically active or express feelings that are bottled up: run around the block, tell jokes or funny stories and laugh, and then return to the decision.

- Have your child role-play each of the options and notice how she feels.

- Support your child to physically begin one of the options, or to go to the place where it would occur and notice how he feels.

- Encourage your child to be alone while thinking about the options, in order to get clearer about his own feelings.

- Listen to your child talk about each of the options. Suggest that your child write or draw. Notice how each sounds or looks to her.

- Suggest that your child unwind in a daydream, in silence, or by humming, and notice what other ideas emerge.

Visual In the Mud

- Gets overwhelmed by many inner images, not knowing which to draw, write about, or do

- Sees the rightness of different perspectives, points of view

- Gets confused when inner images and outer reality don't match

Suggestions:

- Help your child isolate options and imagine each one in detail. Have her notice how she feels, and what she thinks when she imagines each one.

- Suggest that your child write a story about choosing each option. What would happen in each scenario?

- Have her write out a list of pros and cons for each option.

- Collect pictures and written material about each option together.

- If it's possible, go together to see each of the options, real and in the world.

- Have your child choose one option and do it for a short time so that he can notice how he feels.

- Have your child talk with you or someone else as if she had chosen one option and notice how it sounds to her.

- Suggest that your child unwind in silence or with favorite music, notice other options that emerge.

- Suggest that your child unwind with a calming physical activity or rest, and notice other ideas that emerge.

Auditory In the Mud

- Gets overwhelmed by inner dialogue, the inner debate about possible ways to think about a topic, possible words to say

- Says one thing, then another, believing both at the same time, even if contradictory

- Gets confused by others' opinions, needs to figure out what she thinks

Suggestions:

- Ask your child simple clarifying questions: What is this about? What is your opinion?

- Encourage your child to fully talk about the possible ways to think about the topic, imagining how each would feel and/or look.

- Have her practice giving a report several times, and notice which words sound better.

- Ask her to give each side of the story a different voice, then to write down the dialogue between them and act out their interactions.

- Have your child walk or doodle on her own for a few minutes. Notice what words come, what new options emerge.

"Going Around in Circles": Stuck in Expanded Attention

As her brother hits her on the arm for the fourth time, Robin finally loses it. Homework is usually easy for her, but tonight she can't even decide which assignment to do first. Jeremy stares at the computer screen, unable to get beyond his first line of writing. It's not that he has no ideas; he has too many. Winston settles into his third spot of the evening. He can't find anywhere in the house that's quiet enough for him to think. All of these kids are "Going Around in Circles." This kind of stuckness involves the channel of our expanded attention, the one that helps us generate new ideas. This creative mental energy is vital to our learning process, but sometimes too much of it can be frustrating. These kids are being triggered into too much spaciness and can't seem to find their way out. How can you support them?

Three kinds of suggestions follow for helping your kids stop Going Around in Circles. Sometimes kids get stuck here because they're getting too much input from the outside world in their expanded channel. You can help them to take space and protect themselves from the unwanted triggering. Second, sometimes kids get too expanded in the midst of a homework project; getting active can break the spell of too many ideas coming in. Finally, using the other two channels can help your child's mind to balance and get unstuck. Try some of the specific, channel-related suggestions that follow.

Kinesthetic Going Around in Circles

- Gets overwhelmed by too many feelings, being in the presence of a lot of physical energy, unexpected or unwanted touch or physical closeness

- Mind generates too many things to do or ways things could be done

Suggestions:

- Help your child find space where he can be alone, so that feeling safe and noticing his own feelings is possible.

- Suggest actions or movements, to reduce spaciness. Stretch, walk, hop, skip. Choose any activity that would be comfortable and fun for your child.

- Suggest that she walk, talk, write, and get active. Encourage your child to use you or someone else as a sounding board to talk about her options, discovering what's important and realistic about each, and write down the ones that make sense.

- Help your child sort through the ideas that have popped up, imagining each one, and using pro and con lists or drawings to discover which ones are worth pursuing.

Visual Going Around in Circles

- Gets overwhelmed by too much visual stimulation, prolonged eye contact from others or the request to maintain it

- Mind generates too many internal images of possibilities

Suggestions:

- Encourage your child to close her eyes, to look where she wants to, or to protect her eyes and privacy with sunglasses, a hat, or a visor.

- Suggest that your child write, draw, doodle, or paint. Get active visually in a comfortable way.

- Talk or make up songs about options, discovering which ones are practical, which ones feel right to your child.

- Encourage him to role-play options, find out which ones sound good and feel right.

Auditory Going Around in Circles

- Gets overwhelmed by too many sounds, voices, questions, requests for spoken responses

- Mind generates too many words, ideas, sounds

Suggestions:

- Help your child find or create a quiet space.

- Suggest that she talk, make noise, or hum to herself, using her auditory channel in pleasurable active ways.

- Help your child act out his favorites of the options generated; which ones feel right?

- Encourage your child to create inner movies, models or diagrams of her options, discovering what is important and realistic about each, noticing how each feels and sounds.

I hope you never have to use this chapter. This is the part of this book that's a lot like the "troubleshooting" section of my computer manual. Mostly, I operate my machine well on my own; I can figure things out and learn as I go. But when I get stuck, I'm sure glad to know that section's there. If you get stuck, you'll probably find a different kind of comfort and companionship here. As your awareness grows, I hope you'll feel more confident to find your own ways through. And may this be so for your child as well.

Help her to recognize her own familiar stuck places and to find her own pathways out.

Reflection

* *What have you learned about the typical ways your child gets stuck doing homework?*

* *What do you think are the most effective ways to help him when he's stuck?*

* *How could what you've discovered help your child with other interests?*

What is of greatest consequence in a person's life is not just the nature and extent of his or her experiences but what has been learned from them."

—Norman Cousins

CHAPTER 10

Calling It a Night: Learning as Its Own Reward

Sometimes the most important minutes of a night's homework session are the last ones. Making the decision to call it a night, assessing how things went, and reflecting on what has been learned are activities that hold some of the most significant, long-term learnings of all.

Take time to think about how your evenings come to a close:

- How often does your child finish her homework with time to spare?

- How often does she work past bedtime in order to finish?

- How often does your child leave homework undone?

- Who decides whether your child should stay up late or leave things unfinished?

- In what kinds of outside activities has your child been motivated to push himself to finish a task or keep a commitment?

- In what kinds of activities has he stopped before finishing?

- What kinds of assignments seem important to your child to do well?

- On what kinds of assignments does your child do the minimum required?

- How do you support your child to do her best work?

- Do you help your child check her work? Does she do this on her own?

- How important are grades to your child?

- How important are grades to you?

- How does a homework session usually end at your house?

- How and when does your child reflect on what he's accomplished?

- How does your child usually feel about his homework overall?

- How do you usually feel at the end of a session together?

Calling It a Night

When the last stroke of the pencil lands on the page, Brian can't wait to throw everything into his backpack and move on to the rest of his evening. He's always happy if there's time enough to kick back, watch a little TV, zone out before bedtime. I understand the feeling totally. These are the nights when I feel lucky, when there is breathing room around Brian's homework, when he's managed to get it all finished between school dismissal and bedtime.

There have been some nights, and I expect there will be others to come, when the time required to finish is more than the hours we've got. Sometimes, with fairly accurate time planning, we can anticipate the extra time needed, set priorities, and sequence assignments to make the most of the evening's time. On other nights, we get caught off guard by an assignment that greatly exceeds our time estimates and find ourselves with a long way to go at bedtime. How do we cope with this? What are our options? How do we know when it's time for our kids to stop? When should we encourage them to push through and finish? Who decides?

This last question seems to be an important one. It's never too early to help your child begin to take on the responsibility for these decisions. "Can I be done now?" lays it all on you. One of the qualities we can nurture in our kids is the ability to do a good job and to know when to stop. We can help them grow in self-knowledge and in self-regulation. They can develop the signals that help them know when they can meet a challenge and when they've had enough.

At Brian's middle school, the kids are allotted five homework coupons at the beginning of each term. These allow them to have an extra day to complete five different homework assignments of their choice without penalty. At the end of the term, kids who have not used their coupons can turn them in for extra credit. This seems to be conveying an important message—that teachers understand that there are times when homework just can't hap-pen on a particular night or in a particular subject. This offering encourages the student to become aware of when they really do need more time to complete something. What kind of an assign-ment might prompt your child to use a coupon?

A few weeks ago, Brian was struggling to put together the out-line for his first research paper. This had been a long and tedious evening of gathering information from two or three sources. He was most of the way through the process when he announced that he was done for the night. A part of me squirmed, wanting him to just stay with it and get the assignment over with. But Brian was clear; he said that he could deal with the teacher seeing this paper unfinished but he couldn't deal with squeezing his brain for one more ounce of information. How did he know? What I had noticed was that in the final ten minutes, I was doing most of the work. His attention span was down to about thirty seconds. He couldn't verbally track on even one sentence at a time. He was fidgety, trying to keep himself alert, but even that wasn't working. Brian had reached his own limits. Important learning came from talking together about what I observed and what it felt like to him to be "done." Through our conversation, we made the signals of his saturation point conscious to him and to me. Hopefully, he'll be able to recognize these signals when he reaches that point again.

These kinds of conversations can help your child begin to decide what to do when there's too much to do. Offer your own observations and help your child recognize the point in the evening when all of the unwinding and concentrating strategies are no longer working. When your child is close to being too tired to continue, ask her what she is noticing in her body. Help her learn to stop before she is completely out of physical and mental energy.

Sometimes pushing ourselves a little is necessary to finish important things in a timely manner. Help your children become aware of the signals that indicate they could see things through to the end. Help them recognize the qualities of a "second wind." Point out the things that work to refresh them the most when their energy lags.

Whether your child has decided to work to completion or to stop before finishing, assist her in developing some balance between an awareness of her inside signals and a realistic view of the consequences at school. Here are some questions you could ask your child in thinking about when to call it a night:

Knowing It's Time to Stop

- What tasks have you completed tonight?

- On which incomplete assignments have you gone as far as

you were able to on your own? Would you like help to complete these tonight? What kind of help? From whom?

- Have you run out of energy? Is it more important to stop and rest than to finish?

- What will be the benefits of stopping now? How will you feel about where you've stopped when you're in class tomorrow?

- What will be the consequences of stopping now? What problems might arise out of not completing this assignment?

- Have you run out of time? Is it more important to you to finish than to go to bed on time?

- What will be the benefits of finishing this now? How will you feel if you complete this assignment?

- What will be the down side of finishing this now? How will you feel if you get less sleep than usual tonight?

Assessing the Night's Work

Once your child has made a decision to stop whether the assignments are complete or not, don't close up shop yet. Make sure that you take what we call a "satisfaction stop." Pause for another few minutes to review the night together, maybe over a celebratory snack. Some of the most important moments of learning can happen when your child thinks back on what has just happened while it's still fresh. Reflection will help the lessons from both content and process become apparent and useful. It's important to take stock of what has worked and what has not. This process will help your child develop the skills of self-evaluation. It will place the focus on what and how she is learning rather than on the grade or other assessment that comes from the outside. Here are some questions you could think about together:

How Did You Do?

- On a scale of 1 to 10, how do you rate your work tonight overall? Why do you give yourself that rating?

- How does what you did compare with what you had planned?

- How accurate were your time estimates? Did you finish the most important tasks?

- What do you like about what you produced?

- What are you most proud of? What did you do well?

- What was the hardest part? When did you get stuck?

- How did you help yourself get unstuck?

- How did you have fun?

Reflecting on What You've Learned

Revisit the "No Matter What" list your child set for himself at the beginning of the homework session:

- In what ways did you learn what you wanted to in this session?

- What new information have you learned? What will you remember?

- What skills have you practiced?

- How have you shown what you've been learning?

- What have you learned about yourself as a learner?

I have been pleased by the awareness Brian is developing about himself, about his process, and about his own learning needs. Some quotes:

- "I wish I had read that second question more carefully when I first looked at the assignment. It would have saved me a lot of time. I like to think about things before I have to write the answer right away."

- "The numbers on that math sheet were way too small."

- "I realized it helps me to stand up at the table when I do art projects."

- "It still takes me so long to write out my final draft. I'm glad I'm learning to type in computer class."

In addition to your nightly reflections, perhaps once a week or once a month, take some time together to think about what your child is learning and how it relates to her gifts and interests. Pause together and notice when her school work has been fun and meaningful. Notice what has delighted and surprised her, what has stretched her thinking and her knowledge of the world. Tell your child what you've noticed about how her skills are improving in reading or math or art. Help her think about what she is doing well, not just in school, but in her life in general.

Find fun ways to keep track of what your child is learning. Get a map of the United States or the world and flag all the areas your child knows something about, with his favorite color marking the places he wants to visit. Make a timeline of the growing list of people he admires. Build a sculpture out of the math facts he knows. Make a recording of all of the books he's read, or all the songs he can play on his clarinet.

Help your children become aware of their accomplishments. Support them to keep learning on their own, to dream about and plan for what's next. These are the moments when you celebrate, when you notice that the individual assignments do add up to something. Allow time to step back from your daily routines and appreciate how your children are growing and developing, learning and changing.

Make sure that you, as your child's sponsor, also take some

time to reflect on the effect your work together is having on you. How has your understanding of your child deepened? How have you been changed by this process? Allow yourself a satisfaction stop, too. Give yourself credit for the gift you are giving your children—you are helping them discover themselves. You are helping them find the ways that will support them in navigating through the waters of their lives.

Reflection

* *How satisfied are you with how homework sessions end at your house? How would you like to do things differently?*

* *What signals has your child discovered that help him know when to stop working and when to push through and finish?*

* *How is your child growing in her ability to assess her own learning progress?*

* *What ways have you found to help your child reflect often on what she is learning?*

* *What has been the overall affect of this process on your child, on his learning, on you, and on your relationship?*

*"Education is the kindling of a flame,
not the filling of a vessel."*

—SOCRATES

CHAPTER 11

Sharing What You've Learned: Becoming A Learning Resource

The heart of this book has been a process for discovering many things about your child's natural style of intelligence. At this point, I hope you have a much clearer idea of what your child loves, how he learns, and how you can support him to bring his gifts out into the world. Take some time with your child right now and reflect on what you have learned together:

Learning Inventory

Answer these questions with your child:

1. Interests:

- What are some of your favorite things?

- What did you like to do when you were younger that you still like to do now?

- What do you like to do or think about when you are not in school?

- What do you most want to learn about?

2. Organization

- How do you like to organize your most important things?

- How do you keep track of assignments and supplies for school?

3. Time-planning:

- Name several kinds of assignments: What do you know about how long they take you to finish?

- How do you plan for long-term assignments?

- How do you make sure you have time to do what you love?

4. Time and energy:

- When do you have the most energy during the day?

- When do you feel the most sluggish during the day?

- When is it easiest for you to focus?

- What helps revive you? What helps calm you down?

- What are your favorite energizing and unwinding activities?

5. Environment:

- How, when, and where do you like to study?

- What things in your study space at home help you concentrate?

- What things in your home can be the most distracting to you?

- How do you bring yourself back to the task when you're distracted?

6. Confusion and stuckness:

- What helps you when you get confused?
- What are the ways you get stuck most often doing homework?
- What helps you get unstuck?

7. Making learning stick: What helps you remember what you learn?

- Kinesthetic—reference to past experience, hands-on, whole body, interest
- Auditory—songs, rhymes, recitation, rhythm
- Visual—pictures, words, the real thing

8. Learning enjoyment:

- What kinds of assignments are the most fun for you?
- What is your favorite way to make any assignment fun?

9 . Self-evaluation:

- How do you know when it's time to stop studying?
- How do you know when you can push a little and finish something?
- How do you know when you've done a good job?
- How do you like to keep track of what you are learning?

10. What new discoveries about how you learn have surprised you the most? What discoveries have helped you the most?

When I was teaching fifth grade, one Open House night, I passed out paper and asked parents to tell me what they knew about their child. At the time, I was surprised and dismayed at the number of two-sentence responses I got back. As a teacher, my desire for information about individual kids was real, but as a beginner in my understanding of learning differences, I didn't always know what to ask for. Without a concise tool for data collection, if I had gotten what I'd asked for, I might very well have been overwhelmed by large amounts of information I couldn't necessarily use.

What you and your child have just gathered is what I would have wanted to know about him, had I been his teacher. My experience in working with teachers is that many of them would also welcome what you are learning together. We seem to be out of the habit of true collaboration between school and home. Communication is often reduced to logistical information—"The play starts at 3:00 P.M."—or coping with crises in our children's schooling process. But if schools are going to become more and more effective in meeting the needs of learners, we have to do better than this; we must open a dialogue about the core of the educational process. We must gather and share what we know about every child in our mutual care. Children's lives and futures depend on it.

It may be hard sometimes to know how to approach a teacher with information. Some teachers are more open to hearing it than others. In my teacher trainings at schools across the country in recent years, I have found rapidly increasing curiosity about learning differences. Many are eager to gather as much information about their students as they can. My guess is that for most teachers, support and collaboration from parents would be welcome.

Here's how to get the dialogue going. Find the simplest way to open the lines of communication. If your child has been having trouble in math, and you've made some new discoveries, you might want to write a note to his teacher that says, "I know Lincoln often gets confused doing multiplication. Here's what's working at home. If we use some kind of manipulatives to lay out the problem so he can work it in his hands, it really helps. He can do about four problems in a row and then it's best if he gets up and walks around."

Tell your child's teacher what you are working on. Enlist her support in observing your child at school for more ideas. One parent I worked with told me how helpful it was to find out from a teacher that her child went to the rocking chair every time they had independent reading. It was something they had never tried at home during study times.

Phone your child's teacher and suggest, "Elise and I been working on time planning for long-term assignments at home and we wonder if we could set up an appointment with you to share some of what's working. It might be helpful for some of the other kids, too." I would have gladly received such a communication from any parent. Your child's answers to the questions on this inventory would not only have helped me help her, but they might have given me new ideas to help other children as well.

Understanding that there are learning differences takes us only so far. We need to work together to build our repertoire of new ways to learn and teach. We need to know what works for someone else so that we have more options to try with our kids. Experience has taught me that, if asked, people generally like to talk about how they do things. Many of the ideas we need so much are still undiscovered, still under the surface or kept in secret. Sometimes we develop ways we don't even think about that could be really useful to someone else. Sometimes we keep to ourselves our ways of doing things that are not like anyone else we know. One woman I worked with explained to me her internal color-coded images of each day of the week. Purple days were ones that had appointments; on yellow ones, she ran errands. Blue days were travel days and green ones were days off. Because of her busy life, the combination of colors changed every week. This little mental trick might help your child or your neighbor's child sort vocabulary words or math equations.

We never know what will click for someone else. Please don't keep what you are learning to yourself. Use this inventory as a guide to provide you with topics for conversations with teachers, with other parents, and with your children. Please spend as much time talking about what works as you used to spend talking about what doesn't. Some of the best ideas in this book have come from parents and teachers who have passed on their discoveries.

As parents, teachers, and students, we need to be learning resources for each other. Get together with other parents and children. Have joint study sessions once a month and work with one another's kids. Sometimes it's easier to help someone you don't know well; your thinking is fresh and unencumbered by old patterns. Your child may discover new approaches by working with another parent, too. Pick one topic, explore frustrations, and brainstorm things to try. E-mail each other your results. Plan an outing together and notice how differently you respond to the same experience. Share pointers on time-planning or study space organizers. Learning about other people's workable approaches to everyday learning tasks can help us get out of the straitjacket thinking that there is only one right way to organize, one way to deal with confusion or reading problems, one way to study, one way to approach a subject, one way to keep track of learning. Together, we can discover solutions, rather than despair because there are problems. We can break through the isolation that too often keeps the despair in place. We can all help kindle each other's flames.

We've come now to the end of our journey together. In closing, I bring you back to Dawna, the brilliant mind and exuberant heart who has so often brought me back to the gifts of my own mind and spirit. May your discoveries with your children continue to enrich your life as well as theirs. Many blessings on your way.

—*Anne Powell*

"It's never a failure to not realize what we dream. The failure is to fall short of dreaming all we might realize."

—DEE HOCK

CHAPTER 12

The Greatest Gift: An Attentive Heart

Obviously Annie and I haven't told you everything you need to know to help your child through the labyrinth of Boolean Algebra or the mysteries of literary masterpieces that you encounter on a nightly basis each time he or she sits down to do homework. We have been exploring, instead, a process for having different kinds of conversations, conversations of discovery, that might lead you to a new way of sponsoring the gifts your child brings to the world.

If you have gotten this far, you know that these conversations require asking a different kind of question than "What do you have to do for homework tonight, Devlin?" Or, "Have you done your homework yet, Ginny?" Or even, "Do you want me to help you with your reading, Lester?"

You have been exploring the art of asking questions that shift awareness to your child's natural intelligence and way of learning. In this book, we've shared a process that hopefully helped you understand how to reclaim the love of learning that is your child's birthright.

Now what? Where do you go from here?

Because you've made it this far, it's obvious you care about the quality of your relationship with your children. Because you've made it this far, you also realize that these conversations are not something you do *to* your children as much as the beginning of a transformative partnership you choose to engage in *with* them. The conversations you've had together have dealt primarily with the external experiences of sponsorship. As you may have already discovered, this new partnership requires a significant shift in your own inner experience as well. Delving into two aspects of this change will help you move forward from here: the development of a wider perspective of intelligence, and a different kind of engagement in our children's learning process. Each of these can become a strand in an ongoing weave of relationship that develops as you help your children realize their full potential.

Now What? A Different Perspective

When we hold an infant in our arms, we all feel it—that gaping awe and amazement when we look at the prints at the end of those diminutive fingers and the bottom of those chubby little soles. In that moment, it is as if a door inside our heart opens and we feel a wave of wonder at the miracle of this child's uniqueness and potential. Perhaps, in that moment and a thousand times since, you've asked yourself how you could best cultivate this person so he or she can blossom.

But the door closes. We all forget. We all seem to develop some kind of perceptual dyslexia. We all seem to develop a handicap of trust that limits our perception of the unique island of brilliance each child stands on. We see Jerome as a "smart-mouth" instead of a child who uses words as nutrients, and who may be needed by the whole community to broadcast the messages we all have to hear. We describe Gloria as picky, instead of as a child who loves to probe details in order to extrapolate the whole. We think of Beano as a scatterbrain, instead of realizing he is a boy who thinks in patterns and was born to make connections between things. We describe Megan as too-sensitive because she is concerned with the welfare of others, instead of considering that her capacity for compassion can help the rest of us remember to notice the effect of our actions on others. We call Calvin a perfectionist, forgetting that his distaste for inauthentic expression may serve as a indicator of when we lack integrity.

Developing a perspective of sponsorship means being willing, again and again, to kick open that door of perception and reconceive what intelligence really is. Because we have been so conditioned to equate intelligence with IQ tests, we need to continually remember that each of us could probably develop an IQ test that would portray most other people as dumb or disabled. We could all find ourselves entering a particular room or conversation where we felt completely stupid. When we assess talent without considering the entire spectrum of intelligences, we mismatch education, careers, and jobs. The tragedy is that our children and we—society at large—forfeit the benefits of their achieving truly remarkable levels of performance, satisfaction, and competence in areas they really love.

Honoring your child's unique intelligence means being willing to open up areas of your own avoidance to make sure that you don't miss precious opportunities for understanding his or her particular perspective. For instance, in addition to introducing your child to factual reality, you need to be willing to stretch into communicating in metaphors, stories, and fantasies. You need to spend time processing dreams and feelings—including those beyond glad and mad—as well as to share the learning of simple procedural tasks such as screwing in a light bulb or mixing cake batter.

When my son David was quite young, he used to love to "play" at the computer center of a nearby college. At the time, no one had personal computers or even knew much about them. One of his favorite pastimes was writing programs, such as "mugging," where the player had to explore as many options as possible to avoid being hit. In school, his teachers still lived in the binary world of two choices—right or wrong. When given a test, David would wave his hand and complain that there were many more possibilities than those offered on the examination. As you can imagine, this did not endear him to his teachers, most of whom had never worked on a computer. As I realize now, two decades later, they were attempting to educate him for a world that no longer exists.

Preparing children to live satisfying lives in this fast-changing, highly technical, and exciting global culture means helping them maximize the number of mental options they have for responding to a given set of circumstances; assisting them to follow their natural inclinations of learning patterns; and creating a bridge that will enable them to carry the wisdom of the past into the unknown forms of the future.

Now What? A Different Kind Of Engagement

My husband and I had just arrived in India. I had been forewarned not to give money to any of the people begging in the streets, especially the children, as this would encourage the continuation of an abusive system. For two or three days, I contracted in on myself, ignoring the outstretched hands and pleading eyes. Then one evening I noticed that I had pulled in so far that I was isolated from the experience of a country and people I had traveled halfway around the world to visit. Upon arising the next morning, I promised myself that, though I would give no money to begging children, I would give them the gift of my attention.

When I left our guest house, the first child who approached me was a very thin girl of about six or seven. Her hair, eyes, and skin were all the same dusty brown as the burlap wrap she wore. Her legs and arms were like spindles, and as she came closer, the missing three fingers from her left hand and two from her right indicated she had leprosy. Remembering my morning's commitment, I breathed and scooped her up in my arms. Her eyes flashed as she threw back her head and giggled. I began to sing to her a song I had learned from an Alaskan woman, "How could anyone ever tell you that you're anything less than beautiful? How could anyone ever tell you that you're less than whole? How could anyone fail to notice that your loving is a miracle? How deeply you're connected to my soul!"

As I sang, my eyes began to drip large tears down my cheek. I'm sure she didn't understand the words, but in that one moment, we knew each other completely. With the two dirty fingers of her left hand, she reached over and pinched a tear from my cheek and then brought it to her lips to kiss. For a second, the world seemed to pause, to sigh. And then it was over. She giggled, and wiggled herself out of my arms, not even pausing to turn around as she ran off.

I walked slowly on, aware for a moment of my very full heart. By the time I reached the corner of the street, however, I noticed something else. Inside my head I heard a very distinct voice from the past—my mother—who was warning me in no uncertain terms to wash my hands and face immediately. Didn't I know that leprosy was contagious? I smiled in amazement at the cobwebs hiding in my mind. Still, it did seem as if my fingers were tingling and becoming numb.

The real obstacle to giving of ourselves as sponsors lies not in the nature of the recipient so much as in the heart of the giver. To support and sustain the potentialities in our children, we must be willing to change limiting beliefs, expand our thoughts of scarcity, and allow a sense of kindness to dissolve the antique fears in our minds.

For too many adults, we approach helping our children with homework as a job and duty. Fear replaces love as our primary motivation—fear that the child will get in trouble, or fail, or be unproductive or unpopular. The child becomes aware of the absence of our presence. We become aware of the presence of an absence. When we were children, many of us experienced adults turning their backs on our gifts and sense of wonder. We were "adulterated"—those around us may have looked too soon for the adult in the child. Sometime in adolescence we may have abandoned those very same gifts ourselves. Once an adult, it is very difficult to retrieve the child. When, as parents, we engage with a child of our own, he or she becomes both a way out of this abandonment and a constant reminder of it.

Considering what a small portion of our mental capacity we use, it is obvious that we all underestimate who we really are. The greatest gift you can give your child is yourself. By making the commitment to live your own life fully, to work at continuing to grow in self-awareness, you will create a contagion of curiosity. By recognizing and becoming acquainted with your own gifts, you will be better able to accord a similar acceptance to them. By being in search yourself, you will recognize and support your children's search.

Tell your children they are wonderful. Honor their exploration and struggle. Be specific. Give them help, but only when asked. Pay attention to their process and let the end result be wonderful just because they attempted it. Ask them what they have learned and applaud that. Tell them that finding out what *doesn't* work is just as important as finding out what does. Equally important, tell yourself these same things. Let your results be wonderful just because you produced them. Let the task be worthwhile because you enjoyed doing it. Ask for help if you need it, from people who want you to learn as much as they want to show off. Tell yourself that learning what doesn't work is just as important as finding out what does. And don't be afraid to tell yourself you are truly proud of your willingness to "try it out," no matter how humble or grand, just because it was something you were curious or passionate about.

Musician/mathematician/computer scientist Alan Kay has said that we have become a nation of musically illiterate adults because children are taught the scales before they have developed an impulse to music. As parents, we must re-attune ourselves towards the natural impulse we have for learning if we wish our children to do the same.

But What About . . . ?

At a dinner recently, I told four friends, who collectively parent four children ranging in age from seven to fifteen, about this book, its premises, and process. They were, of course, very supportive and even excited. With the banana dessert, however, as each person imagined living out the concepts and practices I had discussed, two major "but's" were served to me. I offer them to you, with my responses, just in case you're feeling you are the only one in the world who has doubts. Even though we travel this journey of sponsorship on our own, we cross common ground.

> *"But what about 'failures?' Or that behavior that commonly one might call a failure—such as when your child refuses to do homework or stomps off in frustration one night or shrugs at every question you ask?"*

None of this behavior means that either you or your child have "blown it." There is no failure, there is only learning. And that learning—without the interference of criticism—will allow you to follow the grain of your child's natural intelligence. As an example, you might say, with a truly curious tone of voice, "Simon, I'm aware that you've been staring out the window for some time now. Do you think you've been doing that for four minutes, seven or nine minutes? What kind of thinking is your brain doing now? Which kind would be best to do this homework? What exactly is your attention like right now? Be sure you notice the clock and when you're ready to shift to the most effective state to do this, notice how the last period of time affected you. Do your eyes seem clearer, or do ideas just seem to pop into your mind?"

The exact words aren't important. But as kids would say, it's your attitude that matters. Children should not fail. When you're in a situation such as the one above, think of your child as a heat-seeking device or an plane navigating by autopilot—never really going in a straight line, yet ultimately still moving towards its destination.

> "OK, we get the idea. But this is a far-from-perfect world. What about the pressure of other parents and school officials? That's a real challenge. Even if you trust the discovery process you and your child are going through, what happens when you're at a school meeting and another parent or a teacher tries to convince you how essential it is that children have more rigorous homework so they will be prepared for adult life? They will just not understand that developing a love of learning and sponsoring your child's gifts can be as important as perfect test scores."

What I can suggest in this situation is that you not mentally abuse yourself, your child, or your commitment to what you are exploring with each other, no matter what. There, but for your trust in your child, go you. It is said that trees that are strongest at the top are those that are blown by the most powerful winds. Let opposing concepts and ideas be just like strong winds in the branches of your mind. Let your belief in your child and your intention rest in the heartwood of the trunk, where it is firmly rooted in respect and faith rather than being swayed by another's lack of understanding.

In Your Two Hands

Parents and schools are meant to serve the gifts our children bring into the world, to bless them, name them, receive them, delight in them. Children should not fail. If they do, it is we who have failed them. Many of us want our children to follow in our footsteps or live out the lives we would have liked for ourselves. We need to combine these aspirations with a very firm commitment to let our children follow their own stars and honor their personal uniqueness. They need us to love them for this uniqueness rather than for the ways they can demonstrate that we are good parents. They need us to engage in learning about the development of our own capacities and gifts alongside them.

All children have two very special gifts to share with us. They remind us that we too are lovable, and that we too are competent to learn. Engaging in sponsorship means joining your child in such a way that you both feel loved, respected, and eager to explore. The only skills really required are curiosity, resilience, and awareness. Though you may have forgotten to use them, they have not forgotten you. They are a basic part of the human inheritance, waiting to be reclaimed and passed on.

I believe that there is a new song in the air, enticing us toward something more worthwhile than better grades or better salaries. We're all a little weary of the ways we've been supporting our children, and want something better, individually and societally, for them and for us. Following that music is what matters. Whether or not you actually discover them, searching for your children's gifts can mean everything. In the act of seeking, you share with them two precious treasures: the belief that they are lovable and that the universe is a place worthy of exploring where they belong. In exchange, your children share with you their precious presence. As the moon shines with light reflected from an invisible sun, their gift can return you to who you were truly meant to be.

There are times when I feel immense grief as I think about how we so deeply need the vast resources of human ingenuity, and yet how it is so difficult for all of us to nurture and protect our children's capacities. I feel despair when I think about how much we need to liberate the human spirit and how far away we seem to be from that. Watching an eleven-year-old boy arrested for murder on the evening news tonight or reading a magazine cover story about the increase of children with "learning disabilities" causes that hurt to give way to something close to rage.

I breathe, remember that I am more than the rage, and cradle that feeling as I did my infant son. Soon, an image rises in my mind of Janey and Brian and David and Jerome and the thousands of other children and adults Annie and I have worked with who have refused to live in a limited definition of what could be possible for them. That image transforms the rage to outrage and then outrageousness. Just enough outrageousness to believe it is possible that this book might make a difference to you, the parents and caregivers who are reading it. Enough of a difference so you will be able to transform the way that you conceive of and perceive the natural intelligence of the children you touch in your life.

> *We rest on all that has come before us,*
> *our ancestors of so many kinds.*
> *We ask that they may hold us in their blessings.*
> *We too will become ancestors*
> *for those who follow us.*
> *May we offer them our full beauty*
> *and a life of attention and deep respect.*
> *May we offer them the wisdom of our heart.*

> —JACK KORNFIELD

Index

attention, 17, 27, 31, 83–102, 117,
146–7
spiral of, 86–90, 101, 104
taking stock, 84–5, 91–2, 94–5,
98–9
reflection, 102
see also exploratory, expanded
and focused attention
"attention deficit", 83
attention deficit disorder (ADD), 91
auditory, 71–4
organizing, 48–50
receptive and expressive, 72–3
suggestions for learning, 78–80
triggering kind of attention,
88–102
options for study environment,
112–3
stuck and unstuck, 120, 123–4,
126
see also perceptual channels

balancing, 55–6, 60, 63, 72–4,
132

"clay layer", 3
commitment, 29–32, 151
concentration, *see* focused attention
concerns, 18, 24–5, 41
confusion, *see* exploratory
attention
curiosity, 19, 35, 95–6, 98

Darwin, Charles, 99–100
death, 2
deficits and assets, 11–2
distraction, *see* expanded attention
diversity, 9–11

Edison, Thomas, 43
Einstein, Albert, 19, 36, 43, 100
ending the night, 129–36
taking stock, 129–30, 132–3
reflection, 136
engagement, 65–82, 88
taking stock, 65–6
what, so what, now what?, 17,
66–9
no matter what, 68–9
fun, senses and perceptual
channels, 70–82
reflection, 82
learning inventory, 139
Erikson, Erik, xv
expanded attention, 83–102
taking stock, 85, 98–9
described, 98–101
stuck and unstuck in, 124–6
exploratory attention, 83–102, 121
taking stock, 84–5, 94–5
described, 94–8
stuck and unstuck in, 120–4
expressive and receptive, 55–6,
72–4, 80–2

failure, 149, 151
see also mistakes as information
favorites, 34–5, 65–6, 70
fear, 148
Fitzgerald, Ella, 44
focused attention, 83–94
taking stock, 84, 91–2
described, 90–4
stuck and unstuck in, 117–20
fun, 69–82, 74, 88–90, 134–5
learning inventory, 139
see also learning; natural
motivation

Galwey, Timothy, 12
Golden Gate Bridge, 17–8
grades, 130, 133

handicap of trust, 144–5
homework
    as home–work, xiii
    as practice field, 8–9, 17 21–2,
        26, 28–32
    and organizing, 46
    and time and energy, 53–4,
        56–63
    sequencing, 61
    prioritizing, 62
    the one truth, 63
    and what you love, 65, 67–9,
        135
    what, so what, now what?, 66–9
    and all 3 perceptual channels,
        74–82, 94
    triggering kinds of attention, 94,
        97, 100, 105
    finished or not, 129–35
How Your Child IS Smart, 7

India, 146–7
IQ tests, 145
interests, see natural motivation

judgments, 8, 16, 18, 35

Kay, Alan, 149
kinesthetic, 71–6
    organizing, 48–9
    receptive and expressive, 72–3
    suggestions for learning, 74–6
    options for study environment,
        106–9
    triggering kind of attention,
        88–102
    stuck and unstuck, 118, 121–2,
        125
    see also perceptual channels

learning, 1–20, 149
    and breathing, 55
    and fun, 69–82, 74, 88–90, 134
    and sensory input, 70–2
    and attention, 83
    as dynamic process, 86–90, 101
    see also fun; natural motivation
"learning disabilities," 152
learning inventory, 137–9
Leonardo da Vinci, 36

managing time and energy, 53–63
    taking stock, 54–5, 115, 132–3,
        134
    balancing expressive and recep-
        tive, 55–6, 60
    assessing assignments, 57–8, 67
    estimating time, 59–60, 68,
        130–1
    sequencing, 61–2, 67
    prioritizing, 62
    reflection, 63
    learning inventory, 138
MIT Sloan School, 7
mental capacity, 15–6
mistakes as information, 5, 11–2,
    15–6
natural motivation, 1–8, 33–44,
    71–4, 135
    as compass points, 41
    and school, 42–4
    taking stock, 34–5, 37–9, 67–9
    firsts, 39–41
    reflection, 44
    learning inventory, 137–8
"no matter what", 68–9, 134, 150

obsession, 116, 117
organizing, 45–51
    taking stock, 45–6
    as a system of reminders, 46
    visually, 47–8, 50
    kinesthetically, 48–9

auditorily, 48–50
three simple questions, 48–9
reflection, 51
learning inventory, 138
overview, 28–32

Palmer, Parker, 5
parents
as sponsor, xiv, 8–9, 15, 17–20,
26, 29–32, 144–52
goals in this process, 17, 21, 26,
50, 53, 60, 65, 81–2, 113, 117,
131, 133, 135–6
communication with teachers,
139–42
resourcing each other, 142
perceptual channels, 72–82
importance of using all three,
80, 88, 105
triggering kinds of attention,
88–102, 105, 124
and getting stuck and unstuck,
115–27
learning inventory, 139
see also auditory; kinesthetic;
visual
Picasso, Pablo, 36, 39, 100
play, as most effective learning
tool, 74
profiles
Brady, 27, 58, 81, 89, 93, 96,
117, 120
Brian, 23–4, 25, 27, 31, 37, 39,
40, 43, 47, 48, 56, 67, 68, 86,
88–9, 90–1, 104–5, 106, 130–2
Crystal, 27, 47, 58, 80, 89, 93,
117
David, 13–4, 145–6
Jeremy, 26, 27, 58, 72, 81, 86–8,
89, 93, 117,
121, 124
Robin, 27, 58, 81, 89, 93, 94,
105, 117, 124

Saundra, 26, 46–8, 58, 81, 89,
93, 117
Winston, 26, 27, 58, 72, 80, 89,
93, 105, 117, 120, 124

questions: taking stock, 22, 30
joys, resources, and more, 23
challenges, 24–5
what they love, 34–5, 37–9
firsts, 40–1
experiences with school, 43
organizing, 45–6
managing time and energy,
54–5, 59, 61, 115
favorite subjects and interests,
65–6
what, so what, now what?, 66
favorite teachers, 70
kinds of attention, 84–5, 91–2,
94–5, 98–9
study environment, 103–4
stuck and unstuck, 115–6
calling it a night, 129–30, 132–3

reflections, 31
natural motivation, 44
organizing, 51
managing time and energy, 63
engagement, 82
attention, 102
study environment, 114
stuck and unstuck, 127
calling it a night, 136
Ripkin, Cal, Jr., 36
Roosevelt, Eleanor, 44, 100

safety, see mistakes as information
satisfaction stop, 133–6
school, 42–4, 150
homework policy, 62, 131
limiting myths, 9–16
Searching for Bobby Fisher, 40
security, 18

self–evaluation skills, 133–6
    learning inventory, 139
sensory involvement, 70–82, 88–91,
    93
Shipman, Barbara, 39
signals and self–regulation, 131–2
Silver Rule, 6
stuck and unstuck, 115–27
    taking stock, 115–6, 134
    descriptions and suggestions,
    117–26
    reflection, 127
    learning inventory, 139
study environment, 103–14
    taking stock, 103–4
    and perceptual triggers, 104,
    105–7
    options by perceptual language,
    107–13
    and classroom, 105
    reflection, 114
    learning inventory, 138

teaching, xv
"tender places," 80, 100

unwinding, 101
using this book, 29–32

Visions of a Better World
    Foundation, 7
visual, 71–4
    organizing, 47–8, 50
    receptive and expressive, 72–3
    suggestions for learning, 76–8
    triggering kind of attention,
    88–102
    options for study environment,
    110–2
    stuck and unstuck, 119, 122–3,
    125–6
    see also perceptual channels

Waitzkin, Joshua, 40

Resources

· · · · · · · · · · · · · · · · ·

Unless otherwise indicated, all of the following are available at your local bookstore, or by calling Conari Press: 800-685-9595.

By Dawna Markova, Ph.D. and Anne R. Powell

How Your Child IS Smart: *A Life-Changing Approach to Learning*

By Dawna Markova, Ph.D.

No Enemies Within: *A Creative Process for Discovering What's Right about What's Wrong*

An Unused Intelligence: *Physical Thinking for 21st Century Leadership*
(with Andy Bryner)

The Open Mind: *Exploring the 6 Patterns of Natural Intelligence*
(also available on audio tape from Sounds True: 800-333-9185)

Dr. Markova's Public Radio interviews can be found at the PTP website:

http://www. ptpinc.org

Including Dawna Markova, Ph.D.

Random Acts of Kindness
by the Editors of Conari Press

Kids' Random Acts of Kindness
by the Editors of Conari Press

For She Is the Tree of Life:
Grandmothers Through the Eyes of Women Writers
edited by Valerie Kack-Brice

The Fabric of the Future:
Women Visionaries Illuminate the Path to Tomorrow
edited by M.J. Ryan

About the Authors

Former classroom teacher **Dawna Markova, Ph.D.,** is internationally known for her groundbreaking research in the field of learning. Author of *No Enemies Within*, and *The Open Mind*, and coauthor, with Anne R. Powell, of *How Your Child IS Smart*, she is also one of the editors of the *Random Acts of Kindness* series.

Anne R. Powell has been in the field of education as a classroom teacher and learning specialist since 1974 in addition to conducting nationwide teacher trainings and presentations for parent groups.

Conari Press, established in 1987, publishes books on topics ranging from psychology, spirituality, and women's history to relationships, parenting, and personal growth. Our main goal is to publish quality books that will make a difference in people's lives—both how we feel about ourselves and how we relate to one another.

Our readers are our most important resource, and we value your input, suggestions, and ideas. We'd love to hear from you—after all, we are publishing books for you!

To request our latest book catalog, or to be added to our mailing list, please contact:

CONARI PRESS
2550 Ninth Street, Suite 101
Berkeley, California 94710-2551
tel: 800-685-9595 • fax: 510-649-7190
e-mail: conari@ix.netcom.com
web site: http://www.readersNdex.com/conari/